THE BUG OUT BOOK

TAKE NO CHANCES AND PREPARE YOUR BUG OUT
PLAN NOW TO THRIVE IN THE WORST CASE
SCENARIO WHEN BUGGING OUT IS YOUR ONLY
OPTION

TED RILEY

CONTENTS

A Special Gift to My Readers

Included with your purchase of this book is your free
copy of the *Emergency Information Planner*

Follow the link below to receive your copy:
www.tedrileyauthor.com
Or by accessing the QR code:

Scan me

You can also join our Facebook community **Suburban
Prepping with Ted,** or contact me directly via ted@
tedrileyauthor.com.

INTRODUCTION

"The time to repair the roof is when the sun is shining."

— *JOHN F. KENNEDY*

Reluctant as I am to start a new book with such a depressing statistic, I think this is an important one for us to be aware of as we embark on this journey together: The number of natural disasters across the world is ten times what it was in the 1960s. Changes to the climate have increased the chances of natural disasters caused by the weather, and we're likely to see even more floods, storms, droughts, and wildfires as the years go by. This makes being prepared not just a sensible decision but an essential one.

As you'll know if you've read my previous books, I'm a big believer in bugging in—sheltering at home safe in the knowledge that you have everything you need to survive on hand. That said, there are certain scenarios in which bugging out is the only option, and it's important to be prepared for these too. In essence, bugging out means leaving your home to ensure your survival, whereas bugging in means staying put to reach the same goal. The common mistake many people make is to think that you can choose which option you will take before an emergency happens ... and this simply isn't the case. There's a time for bugging in, and there's a time for bugging out, and by the end of this book, you'll be able to tell—with confidence—which one is right for the situation you're faced with. To be adequately equipped for a crisis, you must be prepared for both scenarios. I cover sheltering in place in my earlier books *When Crisis Hits Suburbia* and *Prepare Your Home for a Sudden Grid-Down Situation*. You'll find additional information about stocking your pantry for a crisis in *The Prepper's Pantry*. Throughout this book, my goal is to help you prepare for an event in which bugging out is the most sensible course of action.

My family is the most important part of my life, and everything I do to prepare myself is to ensure they're safe in an emergency. I know many of you share the same goal, so rest assured that everything you discover here will be useful for taking care of everyone in your household. By the time you finish reading, you'll know exactly what you need to pack, how to prepare your family, and how to assess any emergency situation to determine the right course of action for your family's safety and survival.

Perhaps a recent weather event near you has made you sit up and take notice. Maybe a problem with your house meant you had to relocate while renovation work was carried out, leaving you acutely aware that you're unprepared for an emergency. Whatever the reason, you can rest assured that you'll find everything you need in these pages to prepare your family for a successful bug-out situation. You'll know what to pack, when to leave, where to go, how to prepare, and how to survive in your new location.

I've been studying both wilderness and urban survival for many years, and preparing my family's homestead for an emergency is an ongoing journey. My education has been practical, and everything I discuss in this book has been tried and tested—if not by myself, then by someone whose circumstances it suits better than mine. My goals are to help you put an end to your worries about what you'll do if you must evacuate your home and to leave you safe in the knowledge that you have everything you need to create a solid plan your family can follow if you have to go at a moment's notice. I've found that most books about bugging out focus on what to pack and not much else— my goal is to make sure you have the whole plan and not just a well-stocked bag you don't know what to do with.

So let's start with the essential question: How do you know when it's time to bug out, and when are you better off sheltering in place?

1

TO BUG OUT OR TO BUG IN? HOW YOU KNOW WHEN IT'S TIME TO GO

I first encountered a common problem with the idea of bugging out a few years ago while practicing with my family. The kids were super excited and desperate to know when we could do it for real. It was then that I realized the importance of not only letting them know that we were planning for an emergency (not a family camping trip), but I also needed to teach them when bugging out would and wouldn't be useful. Now, I play a game with them: When I think it might be time for a refresher, I describe different emergency situations and ask them whether it would be better to bug out or shelter in place. They're quite good at it now, and we have some interesting discussions around the dinner table about the pros and cons of evacuating the homestead in different emergencies. I think this would be a valuable activity for many people, adults and children alike. Not many people know when it's appropriate to bug out, even if they're prepared to do it. And that's why we're starting our journey here. Before we get any further into how to prepare for bugging out, we need to be confident that we know when to do it.

WHEN IT'S BETTER TO STAY PUT

Most of the time, sheltering in place is the better choice. You have a right to be in your home, and it's where all your supplies are. No matter how prepared you are, it is impossible to take as much with you as you can keep stored on your property. You also know your home intimately—where you can hide your valuables, what resources you have on hand, and ways to navigate the area confidently. Essentially, there are fewer unknowns in the location itself, so you're already on the starting blocks from the beginning. You know the escape routes (or you should!), and you know the local resources you can utilize; plus, you're around a familiar community you probably know and trust, at least to some extent. A word of warning, though: Sheltering in place requires you to be prepared. You need to make sure you have enough food and water stockpiled to see your family through an emergency, a well-stocked first aid kit and some basic first aid knowledge, and backup sources of heat and light. In my book, When Crisis Hits Suburbia, I cover these areas in much more detail. So, if you're not yet prepared for a bug-in situation, I'd recommend checking that out sooner rather than later.

I would say that for most emergencies we're likely to encounter, the most appropriate response will be to shelter in place. In each of the following scenarios, the specific details will make a difference, and there may be cases where bugging out would still be the better option, but on the whole, staying put is likely to be more appropriate. We'll take a closer look at how to assess each unique situation as it arises later in the chapter.

Viral Outbreak: In the case of a severe epidemic, it could be too dangerous to leave your home due to the risk of infection, particularly if the virus is airborne.

Economic Collapse: Large-scale economic disruption can lead to riots and other issues. If you're well-prepared, you'll be best off staying at home—especially in rural areas. However, you will need to be able to run your home without the use of the grid, produce your own food, and defend your property from looters.

ECONOMIC COLLAPSE

Civil Unrest: If looting or rioting occurs on a large scale, it could be dangerous to be outside. If there's a high level of violent activity outside your home, staying inside is your best course of action. You can always reassess when the initial chaos calms down.

CIVIL UNREST

Chemical/Biological Attack: The air outside could be extremely dangerous in the event of an attack, so this is probably a situation in which sheltering in place is a better option.

Nuclear Disaster: Although it's best to move as far away from nuclear fallout as quickly as possible, if the situation develops quickly and the affected area is large, it may not be possible to escape radiation without putting yourself in severe danger. In this case, staying indoors and riding it out is the best option.

DANGER

NUCLEAR ATTACK

Natural Disaster: Although it's possible to predict many natural disasters, you could encounter a situation where you can't get out quickly enough. If a catastrophe prevents you from using your escape route (and your home is otherwise safe), sheltering in place could be the best option.

NATURAL DISASTER

WHEN BUGGING OUT IS BEST

Although bugging in is a better option in most situations, there are times when it's safer to bug out. You will notice some overlap here with the scenarios in which sheltering in place is better. This just shows that every situation must be assessed on its own merit.

Approaching Natural Disaster: When you know something acute is coming (e.g., a hurricane is two days away from your home), evacuating the area is the best call.

An Unsafe Home: This could be the case after a natural disaster—for example, if your home is flooded or burnt. If you're at risk of domestic violence or are concerned about an intruder, leaving your home could be safer than staying put.

You Are Cut Off: If you're due to leave work or come back from vacation and a natural disaster has cut off your route, it may be safer to stay away from home for a while and avoid the danger zone.

Notification of a FEMA Camp: If government broadcasts tell you that no help will be sent to your area and specifically advise you to leave, it's time to listen. An emergency camp will likely be set up to receive you in this situation.

Civil Unrest: If looting or rioting is happening a little further away from your home and you can evacuate safely, bugging out will keep you safe if the violence moves closer to where you are.

Civil War: If the whole country is affected by civil war, the safest place may not be within the country. I'd recommend ensuring everyone in your family has a current passport and that you have funds secured to finance an overseas trip if necessary. Bear in mind, however, that you need a plan for this situation. It's crucial to know where you're going and that you'll have safe accommodation when you get there.

Nuclear War: Unless it's unsafe to evacuate the area without the risk of radiation poisoning, leaving your home for a fallout shelter will be your best course of action in a nuclear war. Timing is crucial, however, and you'll need to make sure you arrive at your destination before there's a risk that you could be exposed to radioactive fallout. If this is a risk, sheltering in place may be the better option.

BUG IN OR BUG OUT—HOW TO DECIDE

To determine the right time to bug out, you can use the REDOUT rule. Consider these six factors:

- **R**esources
- **E**nvironment
- **D**estination
- **O**verwhelming force
- **U**nprepared
- **T**hreat has increased

Let's unpack that a bit ...

Resources: If your stocks have been compromised or are low for any reason, moving somewhere with more readily available resources would be prudent. We'll look at how to prepare your evacuation route to make the most of this later in the book.

Environment: Keep an eye on your environment. Natural disasters, gas leaks, and radiation can all make a location unsafe, as can riots or outbreaks of violence. If danger escalates near your home and you can still get out safely, it's probably time to bug out.

Destination: Knowing where you're going and whether you can get there safely is crucial. If you have a secure location with more resources than you have at home and can get to it safely, it may be better to evacuate.

Overwhelming Force: Whether due to a military or civilian threat, it's best to bug out in a situation where you're outnumbered or running out of other options. Stay on top of the news and local updates to monitor the situation to escape any overwhelming force before it arrives on your doorstep.

Unprepared: Even the most thorough preppers could find themselves in a specific situation for which they are unprepared. Obviously, the goal is to be prepared for anything. Still, it's impossible to plan for every possible scenario, and if you find yourself in a situation you know you're not equipped for, bugging out may be the better option.

Increasing Threat: A new issue can arise even after the initial disaster has calmed. In the event of extreme rain, for example, flood waters could rise the day after everything had seemed safe. Keep an eye on the changes in the situation, and be prepared to leave if things get worse.

Is Bugging Out the Right Call?

Of course, bugging out is only viable if your family is prepared and their health and fitness match your evacuation needs. If you're a single person with no dependents and in good health, you'll have far more flexibility than someone with a health condition, three children, and an elderly relative to consider. We'll look more closely at bugging out with vulnerable people in Chapter Seven, so don't worry if you have special needs to consider. However, it's important to be aware of what everyone in your household can do.

First, you need to be aware of the fitness level of both yourself and your family members. Consider any long-term illnesses or disabilities among you, as well as short-term injuries that can affect your flexibility. If a slower evacuation is necessary, you'll need to weigh the benefits of getting out early to avoid being stuck against the potential benefits of sheltering in place.

The second thing to consider is the severity of the threat. The more intense or long-lasting it is, the more likely it is that bugging out is a sensible decision, and this will vary depending on your circumstances. For example, if you live in a hurricane-prone area, you're less likely to bug out in the event of a hurricane than someone living in an area less affected by such weather. Both you and your local area are likely to have measures in place to protect against the damage. Regardless of your hurricane experience, however, if you live in its direct path, you're going to want to bug out—the aftermath of a hurricane is usually relatively easy to deal with, but being in the eye of the storm is dangerous.

Last, you must consider how safe getting to your bug-out location is. Disappointing as it is to my children, bugging out is not a camping trip. Deciding to leave puts your family's life in a certain amount of danger. You could be overtaken by the same event you're trying to escape; you could find yourself lost or stranded; or you could run into trouble along the way. Bugging out is only sensible when it is safer than staying at home.

Assessing the Situation

Deciding to bug out requires you to get accurate information about the situation, which means you need to think about the communications grid. Is it still running reliably? Do you have power and cell phone service? Are any TV or radio stations operating and broadcasting safety advice? If you have an emergency radio, can you get alerts from official sources? If communications are down, this is a definite signal that the disaster has had a significant and far-reaching effect. If you cannot get the information you need from where you are, you'll need to find a way to connect with other people—ideally, a government official or law enforcement agent. It could be, however, that the emergency services aren't functioning. Look for signs in your neighborhood that tell you something's amiss. Have you had callers asking for food and water? Is there evidence of looting? Are stores and gas stations open, and are deliveries still being made? Your job is to answer as many of these questions as you can. Doing so will give you an indication of the severity and scale of the situation. If it's clear that things are bad, then it's time to consider whether it's safe to stay, especially if the grid has gone down and you don't have backup power sources at home. Look for the following clues to help you assess the severity of the situation:

- lines at gas stations, banks, and ATMs
- panic-buying in grocery, hardware, and building supply stores
- news reports detailing a potential threat
- increased military or police presence in the area

★ TAKE ACTION!

Disaster Scenario Game

Remember the game I like to play with my kids? You can do that with your family too, and I think it will help you just as much as it will help them. Every time I quiz my family on potential bug-out situations, I find myself doing a bit of extra problem-solving on the sly, which only supports my preparedness. Here are a few fictional scenarios you can try as thought experiments with your family. Feel free to make up your own too. The more practice you get brainstorming potential emergencies, the better.

Bug Out or Bug In?

⇨ There's a hurricane three towns away. Your home is secure, you have adequate provisions, and you're not in the eye of the storm.

⇨ Riots are happening in town, and it's becoming increasingly violent. Nothing has reached your immediate neighborhood yet, but you're worried it might.

⇨ Riots are happening at the end of your street.

⇨ A wildfire two miles away is rapidly spreading, and firefighters have been unable to control it. Your planned escape route is in the opposite direction to the fire.

The decision to bug out is never black-and-white, and there's no strict blueprint to follow. However, knowing how to assess the situation and understanding what your family is capable of will help you make the right decision in the moment. But knowing when to leave is no use unless you know *where* you're going, and we'll look at that in the next chapter.

2

WHERE ARE YOU GOING WITH THAT BUG-OUT BAG?

There's a good reason we're not starting this journey with the contents of your bug-out bag. You need a strong foundation before you even start thinking about your kit. You don't only need to be able to assess *when* it's time to bug out—you need to have a clear idea of your bug-out location and how you're going to get there long before an emergency ever arises. There are a couple of common mistakes preppers make regarding location, and you definitely want to avoid doing the same. The first is heading aimlessly into the hills, hoping to live off the land. I mean, it sounds sensible, but unless you really know the area and have plenty of supplies in place in case the land doesn't live up to your dreams, then it's a terrible idea and can leave you in a worse position than you started in. The second mistake many people make is to shelter in place when the better option would be to bug out—and thanks to the assessment strategies you acquired in Chapter One, that won't be you.

The secret to avoiding errors of judgment like these is to be properly prepared from the outset. That means planning your location thoughtfully and ensuring it's as well-equipped as you are.

WHAT MAKES A GOOD BUG-OUT LOCATION?

There are several factors to consider when considering your bug-out location. Don't neglect any area; remember that you're looking for an emergency retreat to keep your family as safe as possible, and every factor is crucial.

Proximity

Your bug-out location should be far away enough from the edge of the city that you're away from the traffic and chaos caused by many people fleeing the area at once. That said, it should be close enough that you can get to it within a few hours. You don't want to be driving for several days before you get to safety. It's also important to consider gas shortages and look for a place you can reach with no more than one tank of gas. We'll look at route planning in more detail later, but it's essential to have your driving routes planned, and these should be taken into account when you're choosing your location. There may be a situation where you can't drive, which means your destination should also be reachable via walking, bicycle, or motorbike. I'd recommend somewhere that won't take you more than a day if you have a family. (Although, how far away this is will depend on the physical capabilities of the group.) This also means planning for harsh weather, which may well be why you're evacuating in the first place. For example: If there's a river en route, will you still be able to cross if it's flooded? If there's a hill, will your family be able to climb it in icy conditions?

Isolation

Isolation helps minimize your chance of hostile encounters. You don't want your location to be too close to a densely populated area; ideally, you want to be away from roads and railway tracks. Aim for a place with good tree cover so that your lights are less visible, and keep any entrance gates innocuous and fully locked. The isolation factor is a bit of a balancing act. You want your bug-out location to be somewhere remote enough that outsiders won't be able to get there conveniently, yet you also want it to be accessible to your family the whole year round. The level of isolation you want also depends on your group's size. The fewer people you have with you, the more help you may need from others, and being too isolated could become a problem.

Water Sources

No matter the emergency, water is crucial to your survival, and you don't only need it for drinking—you'll also need it for cooking, washing, cleaning, and growing food. Ideally, your bug-out location will have a natural water source like a spring or a lake. Be careful with rivers, though, as these can flood in heavy rain, so if you're looking at locations near one, ensure your shelter is on high ground. If there isn't a natural water source nearby, you'll need to ensure you have a water storage facility, and it would be a good idea to install a rainwater harvesting system. A word of caution, however: Make sure you have ways to purify your water on hand. That may involve water purification tablets, a cast iron pot, a strainer, and a firepit to boil water to make it safe to drink.

Self-Sufficiency

There's always the possibility that you'll need to stay in your bug-out location for an extended period, and this means you'll need to be as self-sufficient as possible. Ideally, you'll have an independent power supply so that you don't need to rely on the grid; you'll find much more on this in my book, *Prepare Your Home for a Sudden Grid-Down Situation*. You'll also want to plant a food garden (this means keeping ample space, fertile soil, and good irrigation on your priority list). You're at an advantage if there's a supply of wild fish and game in the area and edible and medicinal plants for foraging. If you're considering raising livestock, you'll need to make sure you have suitable space and the resources to do so. You'll also need access to firewood, and if you don't have trees on the property, it may be a good idea to consider growing some fast-growing species, like Sycamore and American Elm.

Security

Security is a concern simply because if you're escaping an emergency, other people will be too, and your location should be somewhere you can defend easily. This makes consideration of your perimeter important. Ideally, your site will be on elevated ground (giving you a good vantage point) protected by natural barriers like cliffs or streams. You'll need to secure your perimeter and camouflage your property—including any vehicles you have with you. Emergency exits are also important. You'll need an escape route if your property is attacked for any reason.

Waste Management

This is important because poorly managed waste can lead to health risks. Biodegradable waste can be used as compost, but you'll also need to dispose of non-biodegradable trash like glass and plastic. This means having shovels and space (not too close to your property) where you can bury them. Human waste is the other concern. If you must dig a latrine, make sure it's downhill from your shelter and at least 50 yards from your water source. You may, however, choose something a little more permanent, in which case a compost toilet could be a good option.

Protection From the Elements

A good bug-out location must be safe from all the elements, which will be particularly important if you're escaping a natural disaster. You'll need to be aware of the potential for floods, earthquakes, tornadoes, and forest fires when choosing your location. Avoid floodplains and areas near mountain slopes, and make sure your structure is resistant to high winds and earthquakes. Of course, much of this will depend on your area. Consider the likelihood of each type of disaster, and prioritize protecting yourself against the most likely first.

Longevity

During the planning stage, you'll have no idea how long you'll need your bug-out location. And chances are, if you have to evacuate your home, you won't know in that moment either. It's best, therefore, to be prepared for an extended stay, stocking as much food, water, and fuel as possible within your budget and space restrictions. The beauty of any kind of prepping is that you can always build as you go—that's what I do. In my mind, being adequately prepared means never thinking you're done. There's always more you can do, and this is the same with your bug-out shelter. Start with what you can afford; as time goes on, you can extend it by looking for more sustainable options.

Affordability

It perhaps goes without saying that you need to consider your budget. It's even more important to remember that patience is key here: Survival properties can be expensive, and it's worth looking around, despite the urgency you may feel to get it sorted. Remember that upfront costs aren't all you're dealing with. If you're buying a piece of land, you'll have construction and development costs to factor in and any other features you want to install. Come up with a realistic budget before you start, and look for creative ways to develop it. Be cautious of buying very cheap land or property: It could cost you more in the long run if you have to do a lot of work to make it suitable for survival. You'll also need to factor in stockpiling and sourcing provisions when designing your budget.

Legalities

It's important to know about government regulations and any required permits in your bug-out location. Although these things may not be the most important in an emergency situation, they're crucial to developing the property as you wish. You'll want to check out the zoning laws, particularly if you want to raise livestock or grow crops. The chances are, you won't need any permits for a basic bug-out cabin, but it's worth knowing exactly what the rules are before you start.

Space

This may seem obvious, but you'd be surprised by how many people overlook the space their family needs to be comfortable. Ideally, you want to provide sufficient personal space for everyone; this will be particularly important if you have to stay for an extended period. You'll also need plenty of storage for your supplies and space for growing or raising food.

Structure

Obviously, a significant part of your bug-out location is shelter. You can choose an existing structure or build your own, but it must offer reliable protection from the elements. It should be able to keep your family warm and comfortable and have ample space for storing your water and food supplies. If you're looking for a safe location in an area prone to hurricanes or tornadoes, you may wish to consider underground shelters, and if you're in an earthquake zone, reinforcements will be necessary. There are many different options for shelters, and we'll look at them more closely in the next section, but for most people, a remote cabin is a good option. It's also a good idea to have another shelter you can rely on in the event of an emergency escalation—a tent or an RV, for example.

CHOOSING YOUR STRUCTURE

The best structure for you depends on the area in which you'll be bugging out, the needs of your family, and your budget. There are several options you can choose from, and we'll look at the most common and effective ones now.

Bug-Out Cabin

A bug-out cabin must be safe, strong, and able to sustain you through a crisis. For many people, a hunting cabin is a natural place to start. If you're a hunter anyway, kitting out a place you already own (providing it's accessible and in a secure location) is an easy way to begin, particularly if you're on a tight budget. If, however, you're starting from scratch, before you even consider the shelter itself, you'll need land to put it on. Land can be costly, but if you manage to find some without utilities, you'll reduce costs; I've seen places go for less than $200 an acre. This does mean you'll have to think about utilities on your own, but the chances are, in a bug-out situation, they won't be running anyway. And the bonus is, it'll be exactly the kind of land you're looking for—not too near a major highway and somewhere few people are likely to stumble upon by accident. Before you rush into anything, come up with a water collection plan—whether that's going to be digging a well or harvesting rainwater. If you decide to go ahead and buy a vacant lot, you'll need to prepare the land before you can build or add a cabin. That means thinking about power, water, and waste management.

Once the land is ready, you can opt for a pre-built structure like a hunting cabin, or if you have the skills and access to resources, you could build one yourself. One option I like is a trailer, which you can actually pick up for reasonably cheap if you're willing to put in a bit of work.

I don't claim to be an expert builder, so I won't give you complete guidance on how to build your own cabin. However, I know many of you will have the skills and determination to embark on such a project. There are a few tips I think it's important to consider if you decide to go down this route.

- Protect your cabin from wildlife by sealing or blocking gable ends with mesh screens or sheet metal.
- If you use T-11 siding, utilize construction adhesive to keep your nails spaced tightly to reduce the risk of birds pecking the siding and forming gaps bugs can access.
- Minimize your use of vents, and if you do have them, make sure they're well screened. Be sure to seal the crawl space too.
- If you have a metal roof, be sure to use waterproof caulking so that water doesn't freeze in the gutter and rip the roof off. To avoid ice and snow

building up, locate any chimneys you want to add near a ridge.

- For protection against both water and wildlife, use pressure-treated wood.
- For maximum support, particularly on the roofing, use metal fastenings and screws rather than regular nails.
- To protect against intruders, secure the entrance points to your cabin by framing doors and shutters in angle iron and using carriage bolts. Add an extra layer of security to doors by equipping them with padlocks. Inside, consider adding hiding places to keep your supplies safe.
- Think about the possibility of a longer stay when you design your cabin. If you have the budget, try to include a wood-burning stove and solar panels.

LOG CABIN

RV/Campervan

The advantage of an RV or a camper van is that it can also serve as your transport, and you can move it as needed (as long as you have access to gas and can keep it running). Motorhomes are the most common type of RV, replacing the back part of a van body with a living area. They usually have a compartment over the cab with a bed in it. Campervans are smaller and don't usually have a section over the cab. There's also a third type of RV—an integrated motorhome with a driving section within the living room. These are usually larger and are more comparable to a bus than a car. While the space is appealing, they're quite noticeable and may not be the most appropriate choice for a survival situation. I would say that if you go for an RV as your bug-out home, a low profile is the most important thing.

We touched briefly on using a trailer as a bug-out cabin, but you could also use a travel trailer as a more moveable bug-out shelter. Something smaller that you can tow gives you more freedom, but only for as long as you have gas. These range from expandable trailers to teardrops to toy haulers, all of which can be towed by a regular car. The advantage of these over other types of RV is that you can disconnect them from your vehicle and set up camp elsewhere, thereby keeping a lower profile.

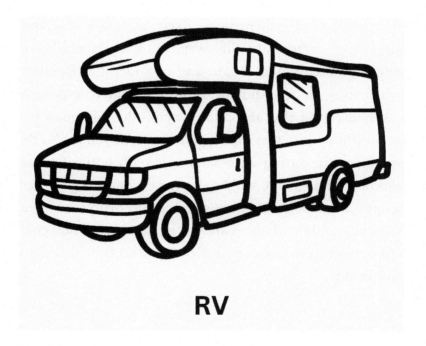

RV

Campsite

If you're using an RV as your shelter, a campsite could be an excellent short-term bug-out location, but I don't think I'd advise it for an emergency lasting longer than a couple of weeks. It has the advantage of being, essentially, a gated community. Furthermore, the other people using it are not only likely to have camping skills that may be useful to you, but they'll have their own shelter, so they're unlikely to be a threat to yours. Often, campsites are set up near a stream or lake, so there's a good chance of a water source. If you are considering this for a short-term emergency, I'd suggest researching campgrounds first. Your best bet is to look for family-friendly sites rather than party ones—you're more likely to find a safe and supportive community this way. Look for somewhere with lake access and a gate and consider the facilities (which may or may not be running in an emergency). Lakehouses are also an option to consider, although it's important to note that unless you own one, you can't rely on getting in during an emergency. With both of these options, although you will be sharing the space with other people, it will be relatively easy to defend that space from intruders, and the chances are you all have a common goal and enough resources of your own not to be a threat to each other.

CAMPSITE

National Park

There are pros and cons to bugging out in a national park. A big plus point is that they've been mapped out in detail, and if you have a map, you can navigate the terrain easily. You can also scout it out well in advance of an emergency, so you can plan exactly where you'd set up camp if disaster strikes. Most parks are protected by conservationists, meaning they still have all the resources you might need (unlike most unprotected land), including water sources. Again, you couldn't set up a permanent shelter like a cabin, but if you're using something like an RV, a national park would give you good options with easy access. This can also be a disadvantage, however, as the more access there is, the less security you have. Aim to find a spot well away from the main roads and trails to protect against this risk.

On the downside, although most people probably won't seek out a national park during an emergency (so your competition won't be too great), most people know where they are, and they could become a target for looters. The terrain can also be rough, so you'll need to make sure you have a safe and accessible spot picked out in advance.

NATIONAL PARK

Out-of-Town Apartment

If you have an apartment somewhere other than where you live, this is a possible option for you, as long as you can get to it relatively quickly. This is assuming the apartment is in an area unaffected by the disaster, though. So, although you need to be able to get to it, it shouldn't be too close to where you live. If you're considering this, stock up your apartment just as you would if it were a designated cabin, and be prepared to leave if the disaster comes closer to your new location. Staying with friends and family out of town is another possibility. Still, the same caveats apply, and it's worth considering how comfortable you would be if you had to continue living together for an extended period.

OUT-OF-TOWN APARTMENT

Abandoned Building

Taking shelter in an abandoned building is a risky option, but it is possible. The main problem is that they're likely to be targeted by looters and other people trying to flee the disaster. What's more, the conditions are likely to be less than ideal. There can be air quality problems, which could affect your health. They may also be in poor repair, potentially making them unsafe. On the other hand, an abandoned building will at least give you walls and shelter and may be a good stop-off point if you need to find shelter en route to your final location.

If you're considering using an abandoned building, look for multiple options, and scope them out carefully. Aim for a one-story building as it will be easier to defend and is likely to be more solid. Try to choose somewhere away from main roads and other buildings that may be prime targets for looters. Choose a small room that you can easily seal off, but try to be near an exit. This makes both security and escape easier. If insulation is lacking, use blankets to insulate the doors and windows, and keep all your supplies with you. Hopefully, you'll have your own water supply, at least for the short term, but in a crisis, you can check the water heaters and toilets. You'll need to purify any water you find in these places, but it will do in a pinch.

ABANDONED BUILDING

Boat

For many families, a boat won't even be a consideration. But if you live near water, it might not be as off-the-wall of an idea as it sounds. While we think of boats as being expensive, you can find them for as little as $50,000, and they come with tax advantages. If you're looking for a transatlantic adventure, a used boat is likely to be a money drain, but as a bug-out location, a boat doesn't necessarily need to be fully functional. Taking shelter in a stationary boat is no less effective than bugging out in a cabin. The only difference is that you're on water rather than land. Many boats have self-sufficiency built into their design. They often have water makers to allow you a constant supply of fresh water; they come with fuel storage, power systems, and sewer systems, which works to your advantage. The fishing potential is good, and it's theoretically possible to keep a container garden on deck. Storing supplies might be more difficult, particularly if you have a smaller vessel. You'll have to weigh up whether you can comfortably accommodate your whole family and store supplies.

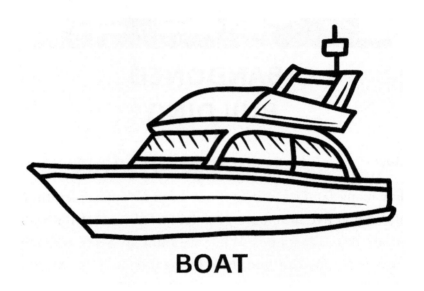

BOAT

Multiple Locations

What I've tried to do here is give you an overview of some of your best options. Whatever you choose, be sure to research it well and weigh the pros and cons for your family. A word of warning though: An effective bug-out plan will include a backup location in addition to your primary one. Something could easily prevent you from being able to use your first choice, so it's a good idea to have a Plan B, with several possible routes clear in your mind. Ensure your backup location is in a different place —and on different routes—to your primary site. You don't want the same thing preventing you from getting to your first choice to be a problem for your second too. My family has a cabin somewhere remote but accessible, but we have a small RV too. The idea is that we can take the RV to the cabin, giving us more supplies and freedom, but if we cannot access the cabin, we can take the RV off in the opposite direction, safe in the knowledge that we have everything we need to survive.

★ TAKE ACTION!

Bug-Out Location Assessment

Considering bug-out locations is no small task. Try using this scoring system to grade potential sites and develop the best plan for your family. The higher the number of points you have for each location, the better an option it is.

Bug-Out Location Scoring

⇨ Easily accessible (no matter the weather)—2 points

⇨ Not easy for others to locate or easily gain access to—2 points

⇨ Several ways to access it—2 points

⇨ Several escape routes—3 points

⇨ Is on or near public, BLM, or state land—3 points

⇨ Strong and sufficient shelter—5 points

⇨ At least one barrier (e.g., cliff/mountain)—2 points

⇨ At least one vantage point—2 points

⇨ Ample storage—3 points

⇨ You can stock it before an emergency situation—5 points

⇨ Near to a water source (e.g., lake/well)—5 points

⇨ Renewable sources of food (e.g., fishing/hunting/foraging/farming)—5 points

⇨ Latrine—3 points

⇨ Familiar area you can find and navigate easily—5 points

⇨ Low risk of natural disasters—3 points

⇨ You know and trust somewhere near to your location—5 points

Interpreting Your Score

40-50 points: Perfect!

35-39 points: You can work with this.

Under 34 points: Major improvements must be made, or a new location should be found.

You'll need to give this section of your plan considerable thought and attention before you're ready for an emergency, but once you have this sorted, you can move on to the part of bugging out that most people think of first: that all-important bug-out bag.

3

MEET BOB: PREPARING YOUR BUG-OUT BAG

Many people fail to think beyond the bag when preparing to bug out; furthermore, a quarter of Americans don't have an emergency go bag at all. Don't worry if you're one of them. You're about to learn everything you need to know in order to remedy that.

WHAT IS A BUG-OUT BAG?

You might hear of a bug-out bag called a 72-hour bag or an emergency go bag. Essentially, it's your survival kit for when your life has been so destabilized that you must leave your home. It will be your kitchen, your pantry, and your doctor for 72 hours—which should be enough time to get you to your bug-out location, where you should have supplies stashed to cover you for a longer period of time.

The actual bag you use isn't important, but having the right kit can help with organization and making sure you have enough space for everything you need without carrying extra weight. The best bag is one you create yourself—tailored specifically to your needs. Bear in mind that everyone in your family will need a bag, as one bag for the whole party won't be enough to get you through 72 hours.

What to Consider When You're Building Your Bag

In order to build a bug-out bag that will suit your needs, you need to know your environment. Your bag is designed to get you from your home to your safe location, so that means knowing your local terrain and any possible shelter you might be using along the way, whether that's abandoned buildings, forests, or caves. You want to think about whether there are water sources on your route, and you need a good idea of the typical weather conditions in the area—particularly if extreme weather like blizzards, tornados, or hurricanes are common. Is there food you can hunt or forage along the way? Are there any likely threats? Think about dangerous plants and animals in your region and any possible human threat that may occur due to an emergency. These factors affect what equipment you may need and will guide you when planning your bug-out bag. However, knowing these things is only helpful if you know what to do with them. If you're unsure about edible plants or how to find water in a desert region, now's the time to research. Along the way, note the equipment you'll need to survive each threat you've identified.

When it comes to the bag itself, I'd recommend getting your kit together first and then deciding on the most suitable vessel. However, I realize it can be a bit of a minefield if you don't know what you're looking for. The best advice I could give you is to read product reviews and see what other customers think. Personally, I have an Eberlestock Switchblade pack, which weighs just over 3 pounds, and has a good number of inside pockets to help you keep everything organized. It has a capacity of 1,500 cubic inches, which should be enough for everything you need. I like it because it's subtle. It doesn't look like a tactical piece of gear, and that will make you less conspicuous if you have to evacuate. On the downside, although it has ample space, it won't support a lot of weight, so if you have heavier equipment, it may not be the best for you. It's also a little on the pricey side unless you can find it on a good deal, which is what I did.

GETTING YOUR GEAR

One of the most important considerations with every part of your kit is weight. I'm a big fan of spreadsheets to help with this—keeping a record of the weight of each item so that you can see how much you're building up. The whole kit (bag included) shouldn't weigh more than 25% of your own body weight (or that of whoever is carrying it). If you can carry less than this, great; it'll mean you'll have greater mobility, which will be particularly important if you're walking. Bear in mind that not everyone in your family will need everything. This means that some of the weight can be shared. For example, one person might carry the camping stove, while someone else might have the cookware. This is another reason I like a spreadsheet for this task.

The best approach to building a bug-out bag is to split it into categories, which is what we'll do here. This will help you keep your provisions organized and give you a systematic approach to ensure you don't miss anything.

Food

A healthy adult can survive without food for longer than 72 hours, but that's no reason not to consider this category carefully. You'll need to keep your energy levels up, and chances are, you'll need more energy than usual. Aim for enough food to last at least three days, and consider what you'll need for cooking; you'll need a few kitchen items as well as food provisions. Bear in mind that although you may need water for some items, it's a good idea to bring ingredients that don't require it—you don't know how scarce water might become.

Of course, what you pack will depend somewhat on your personal preferences and dietary requirements, but I'd recommend packing some dehydrated foods such as dried rice, beans, vegetables, and some jerky. You could also take dehydrated meals, meal bars, and high-energy snacks like trail mix and granola bars. Since they're light and won't take up much space, I think it's worth taking a few spices, too; it's amazing what something as simple as this can do for morale. In terms of cooking and eating, make sure you have utensils, collapsible bowls, and a can opener. Take a camp stove (with extra fuel and a way to light it), a metal cup, and a cooking pot so that you can rustle up a warm meal wherever you are. I highly recommend taking an edible plants guide with you, particularly if you're not confident with foraging.

Water

Water is absolutely essential. Everyone in your family will need a minimum of one liter a day, and you should not only carry it with you but also have a means of purifying water that you find. One consideration you may want to make when you're choosing your bag is whether it has a hydration pouch; some of these can hold three liters of water without the need for extra bottles. Make sure everyone in your family has a water bottle and that you have water purification tablets and water filters.

Heat

You'll need to be able to start a fire to stay warm and cook meals, and I'd recommend taking at least three different ways of doing so in case something fails. Consider lighters, spark rods, stormproof matches, tinder, kindling, and cotton balls that you've already soaked in Vaseline.

Remember that all of these things should be kept in a waterproof container.

Fire isn't the only thing you need to consider in terms of heat, however. Take mylar blankets for every family member, as well as reusable hand warmers and water-proofs. (Rain ponchos are a good idea as they're light-weight and will fold down to a small size.)

Light

Light might not sound as important as other categories, but it's crucial. Whether you're preparing food, setting up shelter, or assessing the environment, if it's dark, you're going to need light. Again, I'd make sure you have multiple options in case one fails. Remember to bring spare batteries too! Choose from flashlights, headlamps, candles, tea lights, LED keychains, glowsticks, and solar lanterns.

Tools

It would be easy to go overboard on tools, so think care-fully about what's essential and what fits within your skill set. Prioritize blades and fasteners; these will allow you to fix, break, or create something you might need. A survival knife or a multi-tool is a must. Leatherman is a good brand, but there are plenty to choose from. An ax is a good idea if you can justify the weight, as it will allow you to chop firewood, and a wire saw could be useful for accessing difficult spaces. A trowel could come in handy for burying waste, and a small sewing kit is a must for emergency repairs. Duct tape and carabiners help fix and attach things, and superglue can come in surprisingly handy too.

Navigation

No matter how well you memorize your route, it's always best to be prepared for the worst. If a road is closed or there's a riot in your path, you may need to think quickly. Make sure you have a compass and a topographic map. I also always carry binoculars so that I can see what may lie ahead.

Shelter

In an ideal world, you'll get to your bug-out location without needing extra shelter, but you don't know what may happen along the way to delay you. Taking something lightweight that you can use in an emergency is well worth the extra baggage. Remember to take the terrain, weather, and any other environmental factors specific to your area into account when you're deciding what to pack. I would suggest a lightweight and compact tent, a tarp or ground sheet, and a sleeping bag and ground pad (for everyone in the family). Depending on your environment, you may also want to consider a woolen blanket or a bug net.

Clothing

The clothing you take is obviously very dependent on your body type, fitness level, and climate. The main advice I can give you is to go for layers and re-evaluate your kit when the season changes. Make sure everyone in your family has at least two sets of clothing so that you always have something dry and comfortable. I'd recommend merino wool; it's comfortable and lightweight while still insulating, and it dries quickly. You'll need underwear and walking socks, and I'd suggest convertible pants and a light, long-sleeved shirt with a fleece sweater or jacket. Make sure you have a waterproof jacket or rain poncho and, if necessary for your climate, a warm hat and gloves. In hot climates, have a sunhat to protect yourself from UV rays.

Hygiene

This is a category that's often overlooked, but it's vital to your health, particularly since you don't know what hazards you'll run into along the way. You're likely to encounter biological elements that your body is less accustomed to, which means your immunity against these threats will be lower. This makes hygiene even more important than usual. Be sure to have wet wipes, hand sanitizer, camping soap, a compact towel and washcloth, and a toothbrush and toothpaste. You'll also need toilet rolls (I'd advise taking two rolls), feminine hygiene products if applicable, and any other personal hygiene items that are essential to you.

Medical

If you've had first aid training, you may feel the temptation to pack more equipment, but it's better to think minimally. Obviously, you want to be able to take care of your family if they become sick or injured. Still, bulky equipment like oxygen tanks will hamper your mobility and is less likely to be necessary for the few days you're in transit. I suggest building your own first aid kit in a light and easily transportable bag. Include the following items:

- acetaminophen
- alcohol pads
- anti-allergy medication
- antibiotic cream
- antidiarrheal medication
- antiseptic wipes
- aspirin
- burn cream
- eye wash
- foot powder
- gauze pads and rolls
- ibuprofen
- ice pack (break to activate)
- insect repellent
- lip balm
- moleskin

- mylar emergency blanket
- needles
- prescription medications to last a week
- safety pins
- self-adhesive plasters
- sunscreen
- suture kit
- temporary dental filling
- thermometer
- tourniquet
- trauma shears
- triangular bandage
- tweezers
- vinyl gloves
- vitamins

Communication

This area can be overlooked if you're not used to prepping. Communication equipment is vital because it allows you to keep in touch with your group, send emergency messages if necessary, and gain vital information about the emergency you're escaping from. In Chapter Five, we will look at "PACE" in the context of transport to your bug-out location, but it's also a good policy to apply to the communication you carry in your bag. PACE stands for **p**rimary, **a**lternate, **c**ontingency, and **e**mergency; in this case, your cell phone covers your primary means of communication. For an alternate means, take a tablet; for your contingency plan, take ham radio equipment (providing you have a license). For your emergency backup, take a crank radio. We'll look more at communication in Chapter Ten, and you may wish to use different pieces of equipment than this, but whatever you decide on, PACE planning is an excellent way to ensure you have ample backup. Don't forget to take solar chargers—your equipment is useless if you can't power it. I'd also recommend a whistle, flares, and a signal mirror for emergency signaling and communication.

Security

As you'll know if you've read my previous books, I'm not a firearms man, and I prefer to steer clear of this topic in my writing. However, if you do have a gun or a rifle, this may be something you'd want to include in your bug-out bag. I do carry pepper spray, and this is all I'd really recommend in this category, besides making sure you're trained in self-defense of some kind (we'll look at this in more detail later). Other things that are useful in the security category fall into other categories anyway—binoculars and a tactical flashlight, for example.

Documents

We may live in the digital age, but it's wise to keep physical copies of some documents, and you'll need to take these with you when you bug out. I'd recommend laminating paper documents to protect them from extreme weather and general wear and tear caused by your journey or storing them in a waterproof pouch. I'd recommend taking the following documents, as well as a USB drive with electronic copies of everything, along with records and memorabilia that are important to you:

- banking information for all of your accounts
- emergency contact information for family, friends, medical and insurance providers, etc.
- financial documents
- ID (include multiple forms)
- international travel documents (e.g., passports)
- legal documents
- licenses, certifications, and permits
- medical records (including prescriptions)

Morale

You can't pack morale, but you can pack things to help you keep it up, and this is important. A positive mental attitude is very important to survival, and there are a few seemingly trivial items worth packing in your bug-out bag to help you keep your spirits up and ensure that a positive attitude stays in place. What that looks like for you will depend on you and your family. For us, tea and coffee bags are a must, as well as chocolate and candy. We always have a pack of cards and a small, light book each.

Miscellaneous

Whenever you try to organize anything by category, some things just don't fit. You may have one or two of your own personal items that you'll want to take that don't fit neatly anywhere, but there are also a few important things you'll want in addition to the categories we've already covered. Consider packing the following items:

- aluminum foil
- cash
- contraception
- eye protection
- face mask
- fishing gear
- magnifying glass
- resealable bags
- salt
- spare batteries
- sunglasses
- trash bags

PACKING ON A LIMITED BUDGET

If you're looking over the list above and having heart palpitations about how much it will cost you to kit out the whole family, don't panic. You can still build a bug-out bag that will serve you well, even if you can't get everything you want straight away. Start with what's already in your house, collecting items to help you cover the key areas. It's better to start with a limited bug-out bag than no bag at all, and you can always add items later as your budget allows. Here are the critical things I think you should include in your starter preparedness kit:

- blanket
- bandages and gauze
- duct tape
- emergency contacts
- flashlight (with spare batteries)
- pre-packaged food
- lighter
- pocket knife
- raincoat
- toilet paper
- water
- wet wipes

HOW TO PACK YOUR BAG

A fully functional bug-out bag requires careful packing, and it's important that you know exactly where everything is and how to access it quickly. How you pack your bag will also affect how well you can use the space within it and how resistant it is to the weather.

The first thing to think about is weight distribution. You'll be carrying a combination of light and heavy equipment, and the best way to manage that is to pack it strategically. I would recommend the following approach:

At the bottom of your bag, pack your softer, lighter items that you won't need to access hurriedly (e.g., extra clothes, a tent, or a sleeping bag). This will be more comfortable to carry and easier to access the things you're more likely to need in an emergency. In the middle of your bag and close to your body, pack your heaviest items. This might include your camping stove or your water reserves. The closer these things are to your body, the less likely they are to impact your center of gravity, making your bag seem lighter. Also in the middle of your bag but further from your body, pack mid-weight items like food and spare batteries. At the top of your bag, add your essential but light gear—rain poncho, fire starters, and first aid kit. In the small pockets on the outside of your bag, keep items you want to access quickly without having to take your pack off. These might include your cell phone, water bottle, and snacks.

It's best to avoid attaching too much to the outside of your bag because it will be harder to keep a low profile, and you're more likely to get caught on branches or rocks. However, if you're taking trekking poles that you'll use immediately, it may be handy to store these outside your bag.

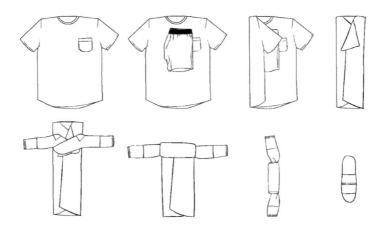

The next thing to think about is how to make the most efficient use of space, and that means looking for hacks you can use to make packing easy. One of the best examples is the military technique of making a skivvy roll, where a t-shirt, underwear, and socks are packed in a bundle. Start by lying the t-shirt out flat. Then fold the underwear in half and put it in the middle of the shirt before folding the sides into the center. Cross the foot ends of the socks over the center of the t-shirt, with the ankles sticking out the sides. Then, starting at the neck, roll the shirt tightly around the socks. You should end up with something that looks a bit like a Christmas cracker. Now, pull the ankles of the socks back inwards, stretching them over the t-shirt roll, making a burrito-like structure. This is your skivvy roll and is an effective way to pack essential clothing items compactly. Another useful tip is to collect smaller items like batteries and matches into a compact container so they're easy to find.

The final thing to consider when packing is the weather. You can buy a waterproof cover for your bag, but it's still worth protecting any moisture-sensitive equipment. Dry bags are useful for this, and they come in a huge range of sizes to cover different items.

EVALUATING YOUR BAG

No bug-out bag is complete until it's been tested, and to do this, you'll need to take it out on the road. I'd recommend four test runs. On Test 1, take a short hike with your bag and assess it for comfort. If you need to make it more comfortable, stop and rearrange your packing, and if you end the trip in pain, you know you'll need to find a bag that fits you better. On Test 2, go for a longer hike, again assessing its comfort and rearranging as necessary. On Test 3, take a backpacking trip lasting between 12 and 24 hours. This time, pay attention to what items you use and how. You may find essentials are missing. Make a note of these items, and review the contents of your bag when you get home. On Test 4, take a backpacking trip to another location. Compare your notes from both trips and look for similarities. Remove anything non-essential on both lists, and add anything you found lacking. Once you've refined your bag after all four tests, you can be confident it will serve you well.

★ TAKE ACTION!

Bug-Out Bag Checklist

It's time to build your bug-out bag. Use the checklist below to guide you, ticking each item off as you find it. Bear in mind that not every item will apply to you, and refer back to the list in the medical category above to get the contents of your first aid kit.

CATEGORY	ESSENTIAL ITEMS	SOURCED
Clothing	Convertible pants	
	Fleece	
	Gloves	
	Light, long-sleeved shirt	
	Sunhat	
	Underwear	
	Warm hat	
	Walking socks	
Communication	Cell phone	
	Crank radio	
	Flares	
	Ham radio equipment (if licensed)	
	Signal mirror	
	Solar chargers	
	Tablet	
	Whistle	

CATEGORY	ESSENTIAL ITEMS	SOURCED
Documents	Banking information	
	Emergency contact information	
	Financial documents	
	ID	
	International travel documents	
	Legal documents	
	Licenses, certifications, and permits	
	Medical documents	
	USB drive	
Food	Camp stove (and fuel)	
	Can opener	
	Collapsible bowls	
	Cooking utensils	
	Dehydrated ingredients/meals; meal bars	
	Eating utensils	
	Metal cup	
	Metal cooking pot	

CATEGORY	ESSENTIAL ITEMS	SOURCED
Food	Snacks	
	Spices	
Heat	Kindling	
	Lighters	
	Mylar blankets	
	Reusable hand warmers	
	Spark rods	
	Stormproof matches	
	Tinder	
	Vaseline-soaked cotton balls	
	Waterproofs	
Hygiene	Camping soap	
	Compact towel	
	Feminine hygiene products	
	Hand sanitizer	
	Other personal hygiene items	
	Toilet roll	

CATEGORY	ESSENTIAL ITEMS	SOURCED
Hygiene	Toothbrush	
	Toothpaste	
	Wash cloth	
	Wet wipes	
Light	Candles	
	Flashlight	
	Glowsticks	
	Headlamp	
	LED keychains	
	Solar lanterns	
	Tealights	
Medical	First aid kit	
	Personal medical needs e.g., asthma puffer	
	Perscription/OTC meds	
Miscellaneous	Aluminum foil	
	Cash	
	Eye/face protection	

CATEGORY	ESSENTIAL ITEMS	SOURCED
Miscellaneous	Fishing gear	
	Magnifying glass	
	Resealable bags	
	Salt	
	Spare batteries	
	Sunglasses	
	Trash bags	
Morale	Book	
	Chocolate/candy	
	Other personal items	
	Playing cards	
	Tea/coffee bags	
Navigation	Binoculars	
	Compass	
	Topographical map	
Security	Fire arms & ammunition	
	Self defense weapons e.g., taser, pepper spray	

CATEGORY	ESSENTIAL ITEMS	SOURCED
Security	Survival knife	
Shelter	Bug net	
	Ground pad	
	Groundsheet	
	Paracord	
	Sleeping bag	
	Tarp	
	Tent	
	Woolen blanket	
Tools	Axe	
	Carabiners	
	Duct tape	
	Knife	
	Multitool	
	Sewing kit	
	Superglue	
	Trowel	

CATEGORY	ESSENTIAL ITEMS	SOURCED
Tools	Wire saw	
Water	Hydration pouch	
	Water bottle	
	Water filters	
	Water purification tablets	

When you evaluate your bag, you may find that you have to make adaptations to make it comfortable and easy to carry. But in an emergency, you have only yourself and your gear. As much as adapting that gear is useful, it's also necessary to train yourself to handle an emergency situation. Luckily for you, this is what we're going to look at in the next chapter!

4

BUG-OUT BOOT CAMP: TRAINING UP FOR AN EMERGENCY

I f you read the chapter title and started panicking about training your kids to handle an emergency, relax. You can actually do a lot of this by stealth. My family really enjoys camping, and I use this as an opportunity to teach the kids survival skills as we go. They love it, and they don't even notice they're learning. Outdoor activities are good for developing health and fitness too. We cycle a lot, and we love days out hiking—the perfect training program for bugging out. The point is, emergency preparedness training can be built into everyday life; the trick is to think strategically about what activities you incorporate.

Throughout this chapter, we'll look at some areas to focus on in emergency preparedness training. As you read, keep each member of your family in mind, and think about what you might be able to do to prepare them or include them in your own training activities.

THE IMPORTANCE OF PHYSICAL FITNESS

It's never a bad idea to improve your health, emergency or not, but if you're going to be able to thrive in the face of disaster, your fitness is important. You'll be less susceptible to diseases like heart attacks and strokes, and you're less likely to sprain or break something if you fall. Simply put, the fitter you are, the higher your chances of survival.

An emergency situation could require you to walk long distances. There may be rubble to dig through, an injured family member to carry, or equipment to move. All of this might be necessary on less food and sleep than you're used to, and the weather conditions might be testing. Stress alone takes a massive toll on your body, and there's no doubt that you'll be feeling more of it than usual. This can trigger health issues you may not be aware of, which you definitely want to avoid. The simple answer to training yourself for this is to exercise regularly. It might not feel like stress in the way you usually imagine it, but exercise places stress on the body, and if you're used to this, your body will handle it more effectively in an emergency. What's more, your body's natural chemical defenses are most effective when you're fit, and your ability to process stored fat for energy or access adrenaline to help you move quickly will be better.

Survival Fitness Goals

When we think of fitness goals, we tend to think about things like the number of push-ups we can do in one sitting or the distance we'd like to be able to run. Survival fitness goals are a little different. There are four overall goals you want to be working toward to prepare yourself for an emergency:

- to reduce the risk of common health conditions like heart disease, hypertension, and diabetes, the presence of which would make emergency survival more difficult
- to improve your stamina in order to facilitate walking longer distances in potentially challenging conditions
- to improve your strength for the purpose of carrying your survival kit and doing manual tasks like shelter-building and wood-chopping
- to improve your mobility to help you move through challenging environments

The question is, how do you know if you're strong and fit enough? Use this checklist to help you. The more items on the list you can do, the more prepared you are for survival.

- Carry an adult a short distance.
- Carry your bug-out bag for 10 hours (walking).

- Complete a day's gardening without hurting your back or joints.
- Escape from an opponent.
- Feel comfortable on just 1,500 calories a day with a high level of physical activity.
- Hike for 5 miles, hunt for food, and carry back your catch.
- Lift and walk a short distance with a 7-gallon container of water.
- Run for a mile on wild ground.
- Swim across a river.

Not all of these goals are easy to achieve in everyday life, but you'll get a good idea of what you can do from comparable activities. Escaping from an opponent, for example, can be tested in a martial arts class. Carrying the equivalent of a hunting haul can be emulated by carrying heavy groceries back from the store on foot rather than using the car. Think creatively, and find fun ways to challenge yourself—training for anything becomes easier when you make it fun.

Fitness Principles and Functional Training

Unfortunately, there's no cut-and-dry formula for fitness training, but the good news is that all you need to do is find out what works for you. At the basic level, simply getting yourself up and moving is a great start. You're not trying to win bodybuilding competitions or compete in ultra marathons. Think about people who are naturally fit and strong as a result of their lifestyle—the stereotypical farm boy, for example, who may not have the body of a runner or a bodybuilder but is perfectly prepped for survival. His body has been prepared by functional work, and his fitness aligns with his needs. Building your general health and wellness is a great thing to do, but it's also essential to think about functional fitness, and to be primed for survival, the best things to do are the things you would do in an emergency situation. This might include going hiking with your bug-out bag, filling and carrying water, carrying your partner if they're injured, or chopping wood.

If you'd like to work on your health and fitness in more conventional ways, this will only be a bonus. I wouldn't recommend making a ton of changes all in one go, though. If you're trying to improve your diet, for example, it isn't a good idea to eat less and better all at the same time as you're unlikely to stick with it. Start by eating a little less for a few weeks, and then start introducing healthy changes one at a time. If you're trying to lose weight, aim to eat fewer calories than you burn and put nutrition front and center. If you're trying to improve your fitness starting from a sedentary lifestyle, begin by walking before introducing more demanding cardio activities. You're more likely to stick to your new plans if you can incorporate them into your daily routine. Small changes like taking the stairs instead of the elevator or parking further away from your office can make a big difference.

If your goal is to work more exercise into your life, choose something you enjoy. You don't necessarily have to join a gym or spend a lot of money on equipment. Plenty of free activities like running, walking, and cycling can make a huge difference to your fitness levels, and these are the skills you're more likely to need in a survival situation. If you have trouble with motivation, try joining a group. My wife did this when she started running, and she found it really helped her.

Last, remember that diet and exercise aren't the only facets of health and fitness. Sleep is crucial if you're to function at your best, and stress will take its toll on both your mind and body. If you're suffering from stress in your daily life, take a look at what you can do to reduce this, and make sure you get 7-9 hours of sleep every night.

Focus on the Big Four

To be at your best for emergency survival, there are four key areas to address. They are fitness, strength, sleep, and nutrition. We've already covered the surface of each area, but let's take a closer look.

Fitness

The easiest way to improve your fitness incrementally is to do more than you're currently doing. If you're relatively inactive right now, just going for a 20-minute walk every day will make a huge difference. If you already walk daily, perhaps you'll want to walk for longer distances or change a few of your walks into jogs. The key is to build a habit. Aim to work hard enough that you get your heart rate up each time. As a bonus, running or walking in your local area will help you learn to navigate the neighborhood, which could be extremely useful in an emergency.

One part of fitness that is often overlooked is flexibility, which makes movements like climbing and slipping into small spaces much easier and reduces the likelihood of injuries like breakages while improving your coordination and balance. This is all extremely beneficial in a survival situation, and it's surprisingly easy to work training into your daily life. Simply by making a 3-minute stretch part of your morning routine, you can make considerable improvements to your mobility and flexibility. Aim for dynamic stretches, which keep you moving at the same time—for example, walking lunges, leg swings, or trunk twists.

If you're like my wife and recognize that a social element helps you stick to your exercise plan, consider joining a club or a class. Good sports for building survival fitness are soccer and basketball, which allow you to work on your agility while raising your heart rate. CrossFit is an excellent way to work on strength and fitness at the same time, while yoga and tai chi allow you to work on your flexibility and balance at the right pace and level for you.

Strength

A common misconception is that strength training requires you to go to the gym, but you can do a surprising amount at home with your own body weight, adding free weights as you wish. The great thing about this is that you can use it to prepare your body for a survival situation, and it's something you can do when you're bugging out, keeping yourself strong and supple throughout the crisis. I'd recommend crunches, planks, prone back extensions, pushups, and burpees. (These are killer and will help you with your fitness too.)

Despite all you can do at home, you may wish to go to the gym a few times a week too. If you plan to do this, aim for exercises that will work on your strength or stamina— think power lifts like deadlifts, back squats, bench presses, and kettlebell swings.

Sleep

Sleep is when your body is able to grow and repair. Hormone regulation and protein synthesis happen during this time, and your metabolism is regulated. Despite its importance, most of us get less sleep than we should. If you struggle with this, try to keep a consistent sleep schedule, waking up and going to bed at the same time every day. Avoid using screens for half an hour before you plan to sleep, and if you must use your phone, soften the blue light from your screen. Finally, avoid eating too close to bedtime. Aim for around three hours between your last meal and sleep so that your body has time to digest.

Nutrition

For some of us, losing weight will help us get our bodies into the best shape for survival; for others, it's simply a case of eating more healthily. If your goal is to lose weight, calorie intake is where you need to look. If you consume more calories than you burn, this will be stored in your body as fat. To manage this, try taking smaller portions or leaving some food on your plate every time you eat. If your goal is to eat more healthily, avoid heavily processed foods or foods laden with sugar. This has the added benefit of preparing you for a survival situation, where the only foods you can access may be foods you can catch or grow yourself. Try to up your fruit and vegetable intake, as well as complex carbohydrates, which you'll find in legumes and grains, and healthy fats, like those found in nuts and avocados. If you're eating a healthy, balanced diet, you shouldn't have any need for vitamins or supplements (unless expressly advised by your doctor), with the exception of Vitamin D. This helps your bones stay strong and is good for your immune system, but it's obtained chiefly through sunlight—which modern life doesn't always allow us much access to. No matter what dietary changes you make, be sure to drink plenty of water throughout the day.

Training to Help With Bugging Out

Whatever you do to improve your health and fitness will be beneficial. Still, if you want to thoroughly prepare yourself for the possibility of bugging out, there are a few specific activities you might want to try.

Rucking

Rucking is essentially hiking a specific distance with weight on your back. In case you were wondering, it has its roots in the military, and the name is derived from the word *rucksack*. You don't need any special equipment—simply a full backpack (perfect for testing your bug-out bag!) and somewhere to walk. Rucking regularly will help you improve your overall fitness, as well as your strength and endurance. Your bug-out bag is a perfect place to get started, but you can buy *ruck plates*, which are weights designed explicitly for rucking, if you'd rather train without your gear. Start with 10-20 pounds, and increase the weight, speed, and distance you walk over time.

Cycling

Cycling can get you a lot further more quickly than walking. The average adult walks at a speed of 3-4 miles an hour, and with your bug-out bag to carry, the chances are, your pace will be slower. The average adult cyclist, meanwhile, can move at around 12-13 miles an hour, and that extra weight will feel like far less of a burden. Cycling as a workout is a great way to improve your fitness, endurance, balance, and leg strength, and if you choose to do this to keep fit, you're preparing your body well for a crisis situation.

Self-Defense

A clever way to prepare for the worst is to combine fitness training with self-defense skills, and this is something you can even sign the kids up for. Martial arts training is excellent for helping them make decisions, learn to focus, and improve their social skills, balance, coordination, and fitness. There are so many options when it comes to martial arts, and there's really no bad choice. And if you're like me and prefer to avoid firearms in your self-defense strategy, training in other means of defense is a good idea. However, if you really want to gear your training towards survival, I'd recommend looking into muay Thai, boxing, or jiu-jitsu.

Muay Thai and jiu-jitsu will teach you valuable skills for controlling a potential attacker, while boxing will help you take an assertive stance in the face of danger. All three are great for fitness and endurance training too. Whatever you choose, aim to practice at least three times a week, and if you can, include the whole family in your training. Keep it simple, and make sure you have a full grasp of the basics before you try to do anything complicated. Eventually, the skills you learn will become second nature, and this is exactly what you want if you get taken by surprise in an emergency situation.

Survival Skills

Before we get any further into this section, I'd like to draw attention to the fact that whole books could be written on each skill we will look at. My goal here is simply to make you aware of useful skills to acquire; I'd recommend taking courses to perfect any of these skills.

Fishing

Fishing is an easier skill to acquire than hunting, and it's possible nearly everywhere. Once you're familiar with the basics, it should be possible to catch a minimum of 1,500 calories a day without more than a few hours of work. Fish have high nutritional value, and if you can catch them when you're bugging out, you're onto a winner. You can consider active fishing (e.g., casting a rod) and passive fishing (e.g., setting up a net). Although, bear in mind that passive fishing is illegal in some places, so check the laws and make sure you have the proper licenses. Active fishing takes more time than passive fishing, which many survivalists feel is a better way to optimize time and energy and can result in a better harvest if it's successful (this is the reason it's illegal in so many areas). The best times of day to fish are in the morning and the evening because this is when the fish come to the surface for food. Look for spots that fish might come to for cover (docks and rock formations are good locations), and look for areas where the water movement is different.

No matter what type of fishing you do or how experienced you are, you'll need a fishing license, which is easy to get and inexpensive. There are different licenses available depending on the state you're fishing in, the amount of time you spend fishing, the type of fish you're targeting, the method you use, and what you plan to do with your catch. Check the requirements carefully, and make sure you have the right license for your needs.

Hunting

Hunting will require a lot more training than fishing. Again, you'll need a license, and you'll need much more gear to get started. I'd highly recommend taking a course if you're a beginner and learning about the safety rules before you start. I thought carefully about what to include in this section and, in the end, decided that the most responsible thing to do would be to cover as little as possible. If you're new to hunting, you need to learn properly, and there isn't space in this book to cover what you need to know. What I will say, however, is that obtaining a hunting license is important, and as with fishing, it will need to be specific to the kind of hunting you're planning on doing. You can get a hunting license from the wildlife department in your state, along with all the information you need to know about getting one.

Foraging

Foraging is a handy skill to have in an emergency situation. You can't guarantee that you won't find yourself lost in the wild or at the end of your emergency food supplies. It's a fun skill to learn, and while you're building up your knowledge, you get to benefit from bringing new flavors to your cooking and trying out new recipes with your bounty.

While there's plenty to be written about foraging, and it wouldn't hurt to take a course, with a good edible plants book by your side, you can do a lot to develop your skills independently. Just make sure you follow a few safety rules when you're out and about:

- Don't eat anything if you're not certain what it is.
- Make sure you're familiar with the environment you're foraging in and be aware of dangers like rivers and cliffs.
- Focus on looking for plants you're familiar with rather than looking for new species that could be dangerous.
- Memorize some of the edible plants that are common where you live.
- Use a field guide to help with safe preparation and cooking.
- Be alert to wild animals when you're foraging.
- Make sure someone knows where you are when you go out.

If you're unsure where to start, your backyard could surprise you. Many edible plants are viewed as weeds, and you may find some in your lawn or local park. If you live in a humid area, you will likely find edible plants in clearings or sunnier spots. If you live in a drier area, you're more likely to find edible plants near water. If you venture out into the woods, avoid plants that are sparse. Plants that grow in abundance are less likely to be toxic and more likely to be edible. Be advised that edible plants often have similar traits to poisonous ones, and sometimes a partly edible plant may have components that are harmful to the human body. A field guide is, therefore, essential, no matter how much you think you already know.

Bushcraft

Bushcraft skills allow you to use the resources available in the natural environment to ensure your survival. They cover a range of competencies, but there are some particularly important ones I think are well worth taking the time to learn.

Lighting a fire

This is an extremely important skill that will not only provide you with heat and light but also with the means to boil water or cook a meal. As with anything, practice makes perfect, and the more you can get out there and practice your skills, the better. As your confidence grows, try to extend your skills, practicing in all seasons and weather conditions and forcing yourself to use only natural materials rather than relying on man-made materials like fire starters and Vaseline. Source dry kindling and wood, bearing in mind that this will be more difficult during the winter.

Tracking

Unlike lighting a fire, tracking is a skill that's easier to practice in the winter when icy conditions make it easier to see footprints, which means that practicing during the summer is also crucial. However, if you're new to tracking, starting in the winter is a good call because you'll find it easier to learn the traits and behaviors of specific animals that you'll then be able to use to help you in the summer.

Navigation skills

There are more horror stories than I'm comfortable with about people getting lost and meeting fatal results because their GPS went down or malfunctioned. If the grid goes down or you run out of batteries, it's crucial that you can find your way to safety using a map and compass. Odd as it may seem, a great time to practice your navigation skills is at night because the limited visibility forces you to take more notice of tiny details and work harder to keep track of your exact location. This attention to detail will be useful if you find yourself in dense woodland or difficult weather conditions during an emergency.

Making a lantern

If you're well prepared, you will have flashlights and batteries with you in an emergency situation. Nonetheless, if you have to bug out during the winter when the days are shorter, you may find a greater need for light and battery preservation. Making a lantern is, therefore, a valuable skill and gives you a backup plan in case your flashlights or batteries fail. There are a few different approaches to this. You could make a candle holder using sticks and bark, or you could use the ends of used candles to make a bigger candle by melting them into a tin and adding a fresh wick. To really go full bushcraft, you could craft a lantern out of only natural materials like birch bark or pine resin. These may not burn for as long as other materials, but you can experiment to find the best options to use in an emergency.

Melting snow to drink

Bugging out in icy conditions is, in many ways, far from ideal. However, snow can be a valuable asset when it comes to your water supply if you know how to access it. One option is to fill a pan with snow and heat it until it melts. The problem with this method is that the snow takes up more space than the water due to the quantity of air it contains, causing a space between the melted and unmelted snow, and in an aluminum pan, this can result in a hole being burned in the bottom. A better option is to add some water (if you have access to it) to the pan first, gradually adding snow and allowing it to melt. This also helps with the problem that it can take quite a long time to produce not very much water when you start with snow; starting with water will allow the snow to melt more quickly and efficiently. It's a good idea to practice this skill if possible, as you'll very quickly see that snow is variable, and each harvest will melt differently. An alternative solution would be to fill a piece of clothing with snow, hang it beside a fire, and allow it to melt into a container through the fabric.

Ax skills

Ax skills aren't of much use to many people in regular life, but they'll be crucial in a survival situation when firewood is critical to your survival. You need to be able to process dead, dry wood into firewood, covering a range of sizes from kindling to medium logs.

MAKING A TRIAL RUN

One of the most important things to practice is bugging out itself. At a bare minimum, you should do a full trial run of navigating your planned route with your bug-out bag once. This is the only way that you'll spot potential problems and fix them before they become a hazard. I'd personally recommend doing your dummy run several times. Try it in all weather conditions and adapt your supplies accordingly. Remember to assess your bug-out bag and make necessary adjustments according to your experiences on trial runs. And a final word to the wise: Be sure to test out all your equipment too. A trial run doesn't just pertain to the route but to making sure all your equipment is fully functional too.

★ TAKE ACTION!

Devise a Training Plan

When there's so much to cover, training for bugging out can seem daunting, and the danger is that you might want to avoid doing it. I'd recommend coming up with a training plan before you start. This will give you something you can follow logically, breaking it down piece by piece. Only you know your fitness level and lifestyle, so this is best done by you, and any template I could give you would fail to take into account your unique needs. Identify what areas you need to work on, and develop milestones you'd like to hit at particular times. Ultimately, it doesn't matter if you hit them on time; all that matters is that you keep moving forward.

Improving your fitness and training for an emergency is sensible, but it won't necessarily be the case that you'll be entirely on foot if you have to bug out. In the next chapter, we'll look at how you'll get to your bug-out location. However that is, this is something you should cover in your trial run. Before we get to that, though, let's take a moment to appreciate what we've achieved so far.

A QUICK BREATHER TO FOCUS ON WHAT YOU'VE ACHIEVED

"Tell me and I forget, teach me and I may remember, involve me and I learn."

— *BENJAMIN FRANKLIN*

Although there are plenty of specific areas to train in, many of them physical, it's important to recognize the advances you're already making. Every new piece of information you gather, every additional thought you give to your bug-out plan, is in itself training.

If you think about any course you've been on that ends with a practical exam, you'll notice that every part of that course was important. You may not have used every detail in the exam itself, but it was that understanding of the broad picture that got you to where you needed to be in order to pass.

So if ever you feel downhearted when you look at the amount of training and preparation still ahead of you, take a moment to appreciate everything you've achieved so far. Even if all you've done at this point is reading, that's an essential step that will allow you to execute every part of your planning process more successfully.

I know how daunting it can feel, and trust me, I've felt it myself, so I try to slow down here and there to share a word of encouragement. My goal is to help as many people as I can to prepare fully for an emergency situation, and that includes every part of the picture.

This is your opportunity to help me...

By leaving a review of this book on Amazon, you'll show new readers where they can find all the information they need to start preparing and training themselves up for a potential emergency.

Simply by letting other people know how this book has helped you and what they'll find inside, you'll be helping them with their own training program—and working on yours at the same time. When we share the information we've learned and think about it from the point of view of how it will help others, we consolidate and deepen our understanding—and that will only serve your preparation efforts.

Thank you for your helping me to make sure this guidance reaches as many people as it can. If you've read my other books, you'll already know my motto: Stay healthy; stay strong; stay prepared... and for that, every one of us needs all the training we can get.

Scan the QR code below to leave your review:

5

WHICH WAY... AND HOW? PLANNING YOUR TRANSIT

We looked at choosing the best bug-out location for your family in Chapter Two, but each option depends on you being able to get to them in an emergency. You should have several alternative ways of getting to each of your potential locations to account for any disaster that may get in your way. You might remember I told you about my family's two locations—a remote cabin and an RV. The RV is both a potential bug-out location and a means of travel, but we have several options when it comes to getting to the cabin. Were we unable to use the RV for any reason, or should the roads all be blocked, we also have two different walking routes that we could use. Additionally, we have bikes kitted out to carry all our gear, so if we needed to get away quickly but were unable to use the RV, we could cycle.

WHY IT'S IMPORTANT TO HAVE DIFFERENT OPTIONS

Someone once told me I was going overboard having this many alternatives planned, but the truth is that being properly prepared means being overprepared. You need to be ready for as much as you can—including things going wrong with Plan A. By its nature, an emergency situation is unpredictable, and you have no guarantee that your original plan will be possible. Some routes may be blocked, either by the disaster itself or by the police or the military. This means it's important to know secondary roads, rail tracks, or lesser-known trails too, and it's crucial that your location be accessible in several different ways. It's also a reason that distance is important. If the only way you can access it is by car, you're immediately cut off if there's something to prevent you from driving. Ideally, you want to plan a route for every type of transit available to you—just as I have with driving, walking, and cycling.

PACE planning, which you may remember from Chapter Three, is a good way to approach this. That means having a primary, alternative, contingency, and emergency plan for both your location and routes. Alternative routes probably involve roads less traveled, and your contingency and emergency routes may seem less than ideal in ordinary life. The most viable route will be your primary route. I'd suggest color-coding your plans on a map so that you can clearly see the exact route for each part of the PACE acronym.

WHAT ARE YOUR OPTIONS?

Before you can effectively begin your PACE planning, you need to know what your options are. For most people, this comes down to five different modes of transportation: walking, cycling, motorcycling, driving, or sailing.

Bugging Out on Foot

Whether it will be possible for you to bug out on foot depends on a few factors, the most pressing of which is the situation at the time. If you need to bug out, it means you have no option but to leave your home, and that means there's a situation in front of you that you must assess carefully. Will it be safe for your family to escape on foot? Is everyone capable of making the journey? You'll need to consider your physical strength and that of your family (and this is why training up is essential). This is something you can plan for to an extent, but if someone sustains an injury in the disaster, you may need to rethink your plans. You will, of course, need to consider your bug-out location too; it needs to be within three days' walking distance, and you need to be able to reach it in potentially severe weather conditions.

If you're confident that bugging out on foot is the right option, you'll need to make sure you're adequately prepared. Footwear is crucial: Everyone in your party needs a good pair of walking shoes, which should be broken in and supported with good, thick socks. Your clothing should be weather appropriate—light enough that you don't overheat in the summer (while still protecting you from the sun) or warm enough to help you survive in a cold climate. You can plan for this by knowing your climate and the changes you can expect throughout the seasons, although extreme weather may force you to reevaluate your plans.

You should know your route and your paths inside out, but it's wise to have some backup routes planned in case there's some reason you can't go with your original.

Once you're on the road, you might find it tempting to press on and get to your destination as quickly as possible, but remember that rest is important. Taking breaks frequently will help you conserve energy, give you a chance to fuel and relieve yourself, and help younger or more vulnerable members of your family gather their strength. If you do need to stop, it's wise to keep someone on guard duty at all times, particularly if you're concerned about civil unrest.

Bugging Out by Bike

Getting to your bug-out location by bike offers you significant advantages. The most obvious of these is the speed compared to walking. It would take most people around three hours to walk 10 miles, but that distance could be cycled in an hour—without having to carry the weight of your bug-out bag on your back. Bikes can easily be carried when the ground becomes too tricky for cycling, and they're quiet, allowing you to keep a low profile when you're on the move. They also offer an advantage in heavy traffic, as you can weave through or veer off down sidewalks or smaller paths. Again, fitness is a must, and if you are cycling with your family, you'll need to be sure that everyone has the confidence and experience to cycle to your location safely.

The disadvantages of cycling are few, but they're worth considering. The biggest risk is something going wrong mechanically, but if you choose the right bike and make sure you have a comprehensive repair kit, you can mitigate most of the risk. Another issue is that if you become compromised, it might be difficult for you to remove your supplies from the bike, putting them in jeopardy of being looted. Lastly, there's the risk of injury. This could, of course, happen on foot too, but with a bike, there's a chance that you could fall off and sustain a much more difficult injury. That said, I don't think any of this is enough to make a bike a bad option; just make sure that yours is up to the task, or buy one with bugging out in mind.

If you're buying a bike specifically for the purpose, the main things to consider are strength and weight. A mountain bike is probably your best bet for survival conditions: It's a comfortable and durable type of bike, and it can handle unpredictable terrain. Be aware, however, that a mountain bike is simply a type of bike, and there's still a lot of variation within the category. The frames can vary widely, and you'll need to choose wisely. The winning formula is lightweight yet durable, and for this, your best bets are aluminum or titanium (although this is a pricey option).

You'll also need to make sure your bike can carry everything you need. There's a vast range of accessories on the market, and you'll be able to find a combination that allows you to bring all your survival gear with you—everything from water to a sleeping bag and food supplies. Saddlebags and panniers should be more than adequate, but if you want to carry a little more, you could also opt for a trailer. Some can generate electricity, enabling you to charge smaller electrical devices on the go. You will also need lights, and to avoid any issues with batteries, I'd advise choosing ones powered by the bike as you pedal.

Make sure you have a good bicycle repair kit but remember that this will be useless unless you know how to use it. Teach yourself how to fix a flat tire, replace worn breaks or a broken chain, and patch an inner tube well in advance of any emergency.

Bugging Out With a Motorbike

With a motorbike, you have most of the same advantages as a bicycle, with the added efficiency of a car. This probably isn't an option if you'll be traveling with your family, but if you're a group of adults and all have the skills and experience to ride legally and safely, it's a good option to consider. The downside when you compare them with bicycles is that they're not as quiet, and if you come across difficult terrain, you'll have to push them.

If you're thinking of buying a motorcycle specifically for the purpose, avoid lightweight engines and small frames: It needs to be powerful enough to carry both you and your gear. Consider the terrain you'll likely need to cross. If your getaway mostly involves roads, a commuter bike may be all you need, but if you need to navigate rougher conditions, you'll need a sturdier model. Check that the parts are easy to come by. If something goes wrong, you'll need to be able to get hold of the parts you need to repair it, and you'll need to know how to do this.

Again, you'll need to accessorize to make sure you can carry all your gear. Choose a bike with saddle bags or to which you can add your own, and make sure you have enough space to carry everything you need.

Bugging Out by Car

We touched on using an RV or a motorhome as both a means of transportation and a bug-out location in Chapter Two, but you may wish to use your car to get to a designated location. If this is something you're considering, I'd advise you to choose your next car with this in mind, as not every vehicle is up to the task. You'll need to make sure it's big enough to carry your whole family and all your gear, and you'll need to know what kind of fuel you'll need and assess whether this is something you'll have access to in an emergency. You'll need to consider its speed capabilities, whether it can get you to safety quickly, and whether it can handle difficult terrain and potentially severe weather conditions. For any vehicle you take, it's wise to be aware of potential maintenance issues that may arise and be confident that you can do basic repairs if necessary. It's also worth thinking about its resistance to damage and how well it will be able to protect you from potential threats. Beyond the vehicle itself, you'll need to consider your location and whether you'll be able to keep your car nearby—preferably out of sight, to avoid drawing attention to yourself.

When it comes to choosing the vehicle itself, a car may be right for your family, but bear in mind that there are a few other options to consider. Trucks such as Fords, Jeep Wranglers, and GMC trucks may well suit a family better, allowing plenty of space for storing supplies as well as carrying everyone. They're also well equipped for rougher terrain, and this may bring peace of mind in an emergency situation. For larger families, an SUV is a good option, again allowing you to navigate difficult terrain and carry plenty of supplies. Campers and RVs, as we've already discussed, allow you to combine your transit with your shelter and keep moving all the time. I certainly like this option for my family, and it's a good choice if any member of your party is less mobile.

Bugging Out by Boat

If you live near a river or a large lake, a boat could be perfect for your escape. Waterways are far less likely to be blocked by traffic than roads, and as long as you know exactly how to get to your destination on the other side, they could be your quickest way out. This option won't work for everyone, however, and it's only worth considering if you live near water and have a safe location on the other side. It goes without saying that you will need a boat, as well as the skills and experience to take your family safely across the water. Unless you're confident in your ability to handle a boat, even if you live near water, it may not be your best option.

PLANNING YOUR ROUTE

Your ultimate goal is to escape whatever disaster is threatening you as quickly as possible, and that means knowing where you're going. This isn't as simple as knowing your daily drive to work. You'll need to know potential detours to take if the roads are cut off or if something prevents you from taking your planned route. That's all a lot to recall under pressure, so I'd highly recommend writing it down or drawing it onto a map. If you live in a city, a detailed map of the roads into the suburbs will be the best choice, but if you live somewhere more remote, a highway map will probably suit you better. If your bug-out location isn't included on the map, you'll need a second one to make sure you can navigate the whole route easily.

What to Consider When You're Planning Your Route

It would be easy to plan a route from home without considering other options, but the reality is that you don't know where you'll be when disaster strikes. You may not be able to account for every possible scenario, but if you know that you're often at work, with your in-laws, or at a particular friend's house, it would be wise to plot a route from those locations too. This may become more complicated if you're also trying to get home to collect your family, so make sure you plan a route that will allow you to do this, circumstances willing. You also need to know your endpoint, and that's exactly why we looked at deciding on a bug-out location before we went any further. Your route will need to take into account the people you'll be traveling with and what they're able to handle, and it will need to account for the mode of transport you're planning to use. Bear in mind, however, that it would be wise to know the walking routes, even if you plan to drive. You need to be able to solve the problem if you break down and find yourself stranded. Make sure your bug-out bag accounts for all possible options—and if, once you get to route planning, you notice that there are things you haven't accounted for, view this as an opportunity to go back to your bug-out bag and make it even better.

Conducting a Route Assessment

To be confident in your route, you'll need to conduct an assessment, for which you'll need a compass, your bug-out bag, sufficient water, and a notebook and pen to keep track of things that come up.

A good route assessment can be split into five key steps.

Step 1: Area Familiarization

Before you do anything else, you need to make sure you're familiar with the area. Identify any areas that may be useful to you on your journey, and make a note of each of them. It's important to do this even if your route won't pass them all; you may need to adjust further down the line. The points you'll need to take account of are your start and end points, any meeting points you plan to include, friendly spaces like hospitals or safe houses, unfriendly places like difficult neighborhoods or places devoid of resources, potential choke points, water crossings, towns, places where you can stock up on food, water, and fuel, and visual markers that you can use to get your bearings.

Familiarizing yourself with the area also means anticipating problems. I mentioned identifying choke points. These are areas where you may need to travel through a narrow space (a bridge, for example). Your route must account for these and include alternatives in case they're blocked. You'll also need to be aware of the potential for the landscape to change in different weather conditions; make sure you plan for all scenarios. If you plan to use side roads or dirt tracks (a wise choice to avoid congestion), drive them regularly to ensure they're not closed off.

Step 2: Identifying and Prioritizing Routes

The next step is to identify different routes between your starting point and endpoint, taking into account areas of interest you've already made a note of and the type of transportation you'll be using. Use your PACE planning to come up with several possible alternatives. Now that you've noted the areas you want to avoid, your routes can take these into account and sidestep them.

Step 3: Documenting the Routes

Once you have your routes figured out, you'll need to document them so that you don't need to rely on memory, and you can make adjustments easily if you need to. I would suggest using both a written plan and visual representations of your routes on a map. Be careful with your written route—make sure you include each leg and make a note of every area of interest. You can also add any notes that you feel are pertinent.

Step 4: Running the Routes

A route assessment isn't complete until you've tried out each route using whatever mode of transport you plan to use in an emergency. Follow your own notes, and make changes where you notice that you haven't been clear or precise enough. To level it up, you could even take pictures of the different points of interest so that you have visuals you can refer to later. A good rule of thumb is that someone else should be able to follow your notes with no previous experience in the area.

Step 5: Completing the Document

Once you've tested your routes, it's time to finish your document, taking into account any new notes you made on the run-through. You should have a map and a set of clear instructions, ideally with photos. Make use of color coding on your map, using this to show different routes and areas you want to avoid. To have complete faith in your finished document, give it to someone else to try out and incorporate their feedback. When I did this, I asked my wife to test out my instructions, and she found a few points where I'd failed to be clear enough. Her input was vital to us having a final document we could really rely on.

CREATING A FAMILY EVACUATION PLAN

Part of planning your escape means planning for how you'll get your family together quickly so you can leave as safely as possible. Creating a family evacuation plan is a must (and you'll have an opportunity to get the ball rolling in the last part of the chapter). Your plan should identify your starting point, potential triggers for evacuation, your destination, the route you'll take and how you'll get there, and the supplies you'll be taking with you.

When it comes to the starting point, it may be that different family members will be in different places. Therefore, you need to account for how everyone will communicate and how you'll gather everyone together. Discuss the potential triggers as a family, and make sure everyone is aware of what scenarios will trigger an evacuation. If your kids are anything like mine, you'll be thrown a few wild cards you'll have to weed out (a tiger attack was posed by my youngest son once!), but everyone's ideas are valuable, and discussing this will mean you're more likely to catch all potential threats.

★ TAKE ACTION!

Create a Family Evacuation Plan

If you don't have a family emergency plan already, it's time to make one. I've designed a template you can use to get you started, although you may want to make adjustments if you think there are things your family needs to know that I haven't covered. Before you get started, conduct a risk assessment, considering each member of the family's individual needs. Your goal is that everyone stays safe, you sustain minimal losses, and you can be reunited quickly if you're separated.

Family Information (repeat for each family member)

🖉 Name:

🖉 Mobile number:

🖉 Social media handles:

🖉 Email:

🖉 Important medical information:

🖉 Other information:

Emergency Plans (repeat for each family member):

🖉 Workplace/school/childcare contact details:

🖉 Name:

🖉 Address:

🖉 Contact number:

🖉 Email:

🖉 Emergency plan:

Emergency contacts (repeat for each contact):

🖉 Name:

🖉 Address:

🖊 Contact number:

🖊 Email:

Emergency meeting place:

🖊 Location:

🖊 Instructions:

Medical information:

🖊 Doctor name:

🖊 Medical practice address:

🖊 Medical practice number:

🖊 Medical insurance provider:

🖊 Medical insurance policy:

🖊 Medical insurance contact number:

🖊 Vet name:

🖊 Vet address:

🖊 Vet contact number:

Other important contacts:

✎ Police:

✎ Fire department:

You have your location identified, and you know how you will get there, but that isn't the end of the story. It's vital that the location itself is well prepared and can support you in an emergency, and this is what we'll look at in the next chapter.

6

HOME AWAY FROM HOME: PREPARING YOUR BUG-OUT SPOT

Your bug-out bag is designed to support you for 72 hours, but chances are, you'll need to be away from your home for longer than this. You can't carry everything you need for an indefinite period of time, so it's vital that your bug-out location is set up to support your family's survival. This means you'll need to equip it in advance or, at the very least, have a solid plan for how you will access the basics. Personally, I'd recommend stocking your location fully—it's amazing how much peace of mind this brings. Both my cabin and RV are fully kitted out, and I'm confident that either could support my family in an emergency. Plus, if we had to use the RV to get to the cabin, we'd have an insurance policy in the form of backup supplies.

THE FUNDAMENTALS OF PREPARATION

It's important to remember that an emergency situation doesn't necessarily equate to the need to bug out. As we discussed in Chapter One, in the majority of cases, bugging in is going to be the better option, so it's important that your home is equipped to support you in an emergency. Prepping your bug-out location should not be done *instead of* preparing your home; rather, it is an addition to making sure you're ready for all possibilities.

Over the course of this chapter, we'll take a look at the essential elements of preparation that should be taken into consideration, but preparing a bug-out location is the same as readying your home for an emergency, and everything that you would do to your home is applicable here. For more detail on each area, I'd recommend reading my previous books, which look in much more depth at preparing your home and your larder. To avoid repeating information (and because each area requires far more detail than we have room for in this book), I have included a starting point for further reading in each section.

Food

You'll find much more detail on this in *The Prepper's Pantry,* and I'd recommend reading this or another in-depth guide to food preparation for an emergency.

Your focus should be on foods that have a long shelf life or are non-perishable and will deliver you nutrient-dense meals, no matter how long you have to be there. Bear in mind that even long-life foods have an expiration date, so you will need to keep on top of your stocks, using them up at home and replacing them with newer items regularly.

Foods worth having on your list include:

- canned food (including meat and fish)
- coffee and tea
- cooking oil
- dried beans
- dried fruit
- dried nuts and nut butters
- dried potato flakes
- freeze-dried foods
- granola bars
- herbs and spices
- honey
- jams and jellies
- multivitamins
- pasta
- pet food (if applicable)
- powdered eggs
- powdered milk
- protein bars
- salt
- seeds
- stock cubes

- sugar
- white rice
- whole grains

Water

If possible, I'd recommend implementing a rainwater harvesting system at your bug-out location. Remember that this must be filtered before you can use it for drinking or cooking. You'll find much more detail on this in *Prepare Your Home for a Sudden Grid-Down Situation*. Unless you know that you have a reliable source of water (such as a stream) near your location, it would be wise to stock bottled water or larger vessels like water bricks, particularly if you can't rely on rainfall in your area. As a rough guide, you will need 3 gallons of water per person daily. My cabin is prepped to keep my family in water for a month, and we have a rainwater harvesting system in place as well.

Power

Again, I'd refer you to *Prepare Your Home for a Sudden Grid-Down Situation* to make sure your bug-out location is prepared to keep the lights on in an emergency. If you can, I advise you to make sure your location can keep you in power even if it is cut off from the grid. Solar panels are probably your best option, but you could also look at wind or water power if the conditions are right. If you're unable to do this, a backup generator is a good idea.

Remember that solar chargers can power smaller items, and heat and light can be generated through fires, candles, and lanterns. Be sure you stock your location with enough fuel for whatever sources you intend to use, be that firewood or gas. You will need this for cooking as well as for keeping warm.

Security

Choosing the right place for your bug-out location is key to your overall security. The ideal location is secluded, has ample tree cover, and is difficult to access (although not so tricky that you can't get to it yourself!). These preliminary considerations go a long way to keeping your location secure. It's also important to know the strengths and weaknesses of your site. If you've already observed that the front door, for instance, is less secure than the one you have at home, take measures to bolster it.

If security is a concern, however, you may want to go a step further, and we'll look at this in a little more detail in Chapter Nine. You can fortify your perimeter by planting thorny bushes and increasing the density of the coverage to hide your property. If you want to go a step further, you could even consider adding booby traps, although this isn't something I've done myself. In my opinion, the safety of the family comes first, and I think there's more risk of one of the kids being hurt by a trap than there is of needing to rely on them to deter an intruder. DIY alarms placed both near the entrances and a little further away are a good way of staying alert to potential trouble. If you have the power to accommodate them, security cameras may be a consideration, as well as motion sensor lights, which not only alert you to intruders but deter them as well. If you have a dog with you, you have a natural deterrent already—I know mine will certainly raise the alarm if necessary (and also when it's not!)

Sanitation

The precautions you'll need to take at your bug-out location are much the same as the ones you'll need to take at home, although there will be some variations. You may, for example, not have a toilet that you can flush with a bucket of rainwater, in which case you may need to consider digging a latrine. There are more details on this in *Prepare Your Home for a Sudden Grid-Down Situation*. The key is to know the limitations of your location and plan accordingly. Similarly, you may have to get creative as far as trash disposal is concerned. Waste that cannot be repurposed can be burned, but be aware that the smoke could draw attention to your location. A trash pit, therefore, might be a better idea.

Clothing, Hygiene, and Medical

There isn't much to say about clothing other than to make sure you have it. The clothes in your bag won't be sufficient for a longer stay, so make sure your family has a stash of season-appropriate clothing at the bug-out location too. You know your climate; make sure everyone has everything they need to stay comfortable and dry for the duration of your stay.

We looked at building a first aid kit for your bug-out bag in Chapter Three. Your location should also be equipped with first aid supplies. You'll need the same equipment you need for your bag, but it's also a good idea to add some extras. After all, you won't need to carry them, and you could be at your location for some time. Additional items I'd recommend keeping are:

- IV kit
- magnifying glass
- scissors
- splint
- wound irrigation syringe

Ensure your location is sufficiently stocked with toilet paper, toiletries, antibacterial soap, and all the cleaning supplies you need to keep your family in good hygiene for the duration of your stay. You'll find more details about essential hygiene supplies in *When Crisis Hits Suburbia*.

Information

You're unlikely to have the internet, and you may not be connected to the grid. For this reason, it's a good idea to keep hard copies of survival books and information at your bug-out location. I'd recommend keeping books on first aid, foraging, medicinal plants, and insect identification at your retreat, as well as maps and guidebooks of the area.

★ TAKE ACTION!

Your Bug-Out Spot Checklist

Use this rudimentary checklist to make sure you've covered all your bases. If you've already prepared your home, this should be easy for you. If you haven't, I'd recommend further reading on each of the sections we've discussed before preparing both of sites. This list is designed as a guide, and you will need much more depth in your preparation.

Food

- canned food
- coffee and tea
- cooking equipment
- cooking oil
- dried food
- eating utensils
- multivitamins
- nuts and seeds
- pasta and rice
- pet food (if applicable)
- powdered milk and eggs

- protein and granola bars
- seasonings
- whole grains

Water

- access to fresh water
- water harvesting system
- water storage sufficient for 3 gallons per person per day for one month

Power

- a way to generate solar/hydro/wind power
- backup generator
- candles
- lanterns
- means to build, light, and maintain a fire
- sufficient fuel for one month
- torches

Security

- DIY alarms
- good tree coverage
- motion sensor lights
- secured doors and windows

Sanitation

- a solid plan for human waste management
- a solid plan for waste disposal

Clothing/Hygiene/Medicine

- antibacterial soap
- climate-appropriate clothing for the whole family
- first aid kit
- laundry and dishwashing necessities
- personal medications for each member of the family
- toilet roll
- toiletries

Information

- edible/medicinal plant guides
- insect guide
- maps and guides of the area
- survival books

Preparing to bug out effectively is a personal journey for every family, but it's imperative to pay attention to your needs if you have vulnerable people and/or animals with you. This is what we'll look at in the next chapter.

7

NO PERSON (OR DOG!) LEFT BEHIND: BUGGING OUT WITH VULNERABLE PEOPLE AND ANIMALS

My children are older now, and well versed in survival skills, but when they were younger, I had to make different accommodations for them. My plans still take into account their ages and capabilities even now, so I'm constantly updating them as they grow stronger and learn more skills. I also have plans for my three dogs. They're all fit and capable, so it's just a matter of making sure I have everything they need, but were they smaller or older, I'd have to make different adjustments. If you have children, elderly or sick relatives, or animals with you in an emergency, your bug-out plans will need to accommodate them. Everyone in your party must be able to get to the location and stay safe and healthy once they're there, and your plan needs to support this.

BUGGING OUT WITH CHILDREN

As you well know, the needs of your children vary depending on their age, and the adjustments you'll need to make for an infant are far different from those you'll need to make for older children and teenagers. I've split this advice into three broad categories, but you know your children. The most important thing is that you plan with wherever they are developmentally in mind. In each of the following sections, we'll cover mobility, comfort, safety, and provisions, and these are the four categories you'll need to keep in mind when you're planning for your children.

Infants, Toddlers, and Preschoolers

If you have a baby, you'll obviously be carrying them. But bear in mind that toddlers and preschoolers have a limited amount of distance in them too, and they'll struggle on rugged terrain, ultimately slowing the whole party down. You'll therefore need to be prepared to carry them at any point that you'll be on foot, and that means factoring in the extra weight when you're considering your supplies. Whatever child-carrying method you invest in, be that a sling, a back carrier, or a trailer, it will need to be both comfortable for your little one and allow you to cross any kind of terrain you encounter. Be cautious of strollers: While they do help with the weight, they mean your hands aren't free, and they may struggle on difficult ground. Before any emergency, you can prepare your children by getting them to practice standing up independently after they fall over, showing them how to walk carefully on difficult ground, and teaching them to climb stairs without your help. These mobility skills will serve them well anyway, but they will also help their mobility in an emergency situation.

An extra consideration you must make with children of all ages is the amount of strange and scary noises they may be exposed to. In an emergency situation, there's likely to be a lot of noise, be that in the form of shouting, screaming, or sirens, which will upset your little one. You can reduce the impact of this by having them wear earplugs or head coverings, playing ambient music to them, or traveling during the night when the noise is likely to be less. The more comfortable you can make your little one, the less traumatic the experience will be, and the easier it will be for you. On the flip side of the noise issue is the noise children make themselves. Infants and toddlers are too young to understand that crying and laughing could put the family at risk, and the only way they have to express their needs is vocally. You can decrease the risk by anticipating the needs of your little one and teaching toddlers and preschoolers signs to communicate. For example, you could teach them to tug your shirt to tell you they're hungry or thirsty.

If your child is not yet toilet trained, you'll need to plan for the disposal or washing of diapers. One possibility is to try diaperless training in advance to avoid this problem. Otherwise, you'll need to plan for how you'll get rid of the waste—carrying dirty diapers around with you is the last thing you want when you're on the move or surviving in cramped conditions. Taking a combination of cloth and disposable diapers could be a good call, giving you more options. So that they take up less room, you can use a vacuum sealer to pack disposable ones. Take zip-top bags to store soiled diapers until you can dispose of them properly.

As all parents know, toddlers and preschoolers can be defiant, and if they don't feel like wearing that raincoat, they'll fight for the freedom not to. That's the last thing you want in an emergency when it's pouring down rain and you need to keep moving. You can reduce the risk of this battle by teaching them the importance of protecting themselves from the weather, reminding them each day that the weather helps them decide what to wear.

As far as supplies go, while babies don't need to be factored into your water provisions, toddlers and preschoolers do. Children between the ages of one and three will need about four 2-4 ounce cups of water daily, and four-year-olds will need five. Toddlers require around 1,200 calories a day, which increases to around 1,400 calories once they reach the age of four. For infants, you'll need to factor in the health and needs of the mother. If she's nursing, it's still a good idea to take formula with you, as the likely reduction in calories combined with the stress of the situation could affect the production of breast milk.

Guideline Provisions for Infants, Toddlers, and Preschoolers

- 3 gallons of water per day for washing bottles
- baby food
- bike seat or trailer for small children (if using a bike)
- bottled water (for formula)
- diapers (mixture of cloth and disposable)
- electrolyte packets
- entertainment
- evaporated milk/powdered milk (to make emergency formula)
- extra clothes
- eyedropper/syringe
- harness
- infant carrier
- infant medication
- infant acetaminophen
- instant/ powdered formula
- pacifier
- pre-sterilized bottles
- prenatal or vitamins (for nursing mothers)
- stroller built for all terrains (if using)
- weather-proof clothing
- zip-top bags for temporarily storing dirty diapers

Elementary School-Aged Children

At this age, children are capable of walking further, but it's still a good idea to plan for a way to carry them if necessary—for example, if they get injured or tire out. If they're light enough, this can be a carrier, but for most children this age, you'll want something you can pull, such as a wagon or sled or a child seat attached to your bike. Make sure your plan includes rest stops along the way so that they can walk further distances for longer. You can get children used to walking greater distances or cycling for longer in advance by going on family walks, runs, or bike rides. Show them how to pay attention to the ground, and teach them techniques for walking on mud or slippery surfaces. You can even practice early orienteering skills at home or in a local park and teach them basic survival skills to normalize them if they become necessary. That can be as simple as letting them lead the way to school, teaching them to pay attention to signs and markings, and pointing out safe places like churches and hospitals. You can also teach them simple safety procedures through fire drills or tornado drills (if appropriate in your region) and show them how to build a fire or a shelter. Summer camps are also a good way for them to pick up these skills.

Again, noise is a concern for this age group. Children this age are old enough to know that things aren't right, which can make them uncomfortable; distressing sounds will only add to this. You can use the same distraction tactics as you would with younger children, and entertainment in the form of coloring books, games, or puzzles can also help during times when you're resting. Don't underestimate the power of comfort items like a favorite cuddly toy or blanket.

As much as noise can be a problem for them, noise is a problem they may create too. Children this age can be talkative if boredom strikes, so plan for ways to keep them calm and engaged. Explain to them what's happening as much as you can, and keep reassuring them that you're keeping them safe, and that's why you're bugging out.

When you're thinking about provisions, bear in mind that your child will be able to carry their own backpack, but they're limited in how much they can carry. They shouldn't carry anything over 10% of their body weight, so you'll have to take everything else.

Guideline Provisions for Elementary School-Aged Children

- anti-pollution child mask
- books, lightweight toys, and games
- coloring or puzzle books and pens/crayons
- family photos
- favorite cuddly toy
- flashlight/headlamp
- glow sticks
- lollipops (to keep them quiet!)
- medical ID

- natural sleep aid for children
- personal hygiene provisions
- ready-to-eat meals
- safety wrist strap
- signaling whistle and mirror
- small backpack
- snacks
- spare socks, clothing, and shoes
- strong wagon
- water bottle
- weather-proof clothing and accessories (gloves, hat, sunglasses, etc.)

Middle and High School-Aged Children

Once children get to this age, mobility is less of a concern. They're mostly able to walk longer distances, and they can carry more of their own supplies. To make sure this is effective, choose their backpack carefully so that it fits well and allows the weight to be balanced. To minimize the risk of a traumatic experience, make sure they have everything they need to feel comfortable. Older kids sometimes want to appear tougher than they are, so although they should be able to pack their own bag, keep an eye out for this and double-check their supplies to ensure their packing is appropriate. Remember that they can be sensitive at this age, and their social life is important to them—no matter how confident they appear, they may become withdrawn and struggle to adjust to a different way of life.

Make sure your child knows the plan and what they need to do to stay safe if something happens. With this age group, you have the advantage that they can be told more about the emergency. Be careful that your reassurance isn't so great that it outweighs their sense of the gravity of the situation. Ensure they have all the necessary supplies and know how to use them if separated from the group. You can prepare them in advance by showing them how to pay attention to their surroundings every day and make sure they can find their bearings using a compass, landmarks, or the sun and stars. Ensure they know how to get home and to other places they go regularly, and check that they know how to access your bug-out location from all of these places. They should also learn to contact a trusted friend or family member in an emergency in case they can't reach you. Make their responsibilities in an emergency situation clear to them, and allow them to take on adult responsibilities, which will give them a sense of purpose and distract them from the things they've been forced to leave behind.

Regarding provisions, most teenagers should be able to carry their own. Factor in their calorie requirements, which can be up to 3,000 a day if they're active (which they will be if you're bugging out).

Guideline Provisions for Elementary School-Aged Children

- alternative way to communicate (e.g., backup cell phone)
- collapsible bike and trailer
- compass
- emergency contact information
- family photos
- fire starting provisions
- first aid kit
- food
- knife (if able to use effectively)
- map
- medical ID
- N95 respirator mask
- personal hygiene provisions
- playing cards
- ready-to-eat meals
- shelter materials
- signaling mirror and whistle
- spare socks/clothing/shoes
- sudoku/crossword/logic puzzles
- water bottle and filter

BUGGING OUT WITH ELDERLY PEOPLE

The first thing to consider with older adults is their medical needs. Make sure they have a list of their medications and know their dosing schedule, and stockpile enough medication to last at least a month (paying careful attention to expiration dates). If there are natural alternatives for their condition, it would be wise to have some of these as a backup too. If any medical equipment is needed, make sure that you have spare batteries and a backup generator if necessary, and if incontinence is an issue, ensure that you have pads to accommodate this.

Mobility may also be a concern. If they use a battery-powered scooter or wheelchair, ensure it's always charged and that you have a spare battery with your supplies. It's a good idea to upgrade wheelchair wheels so that they can navigate rugged terrain too. If possible, carry a spare walker and any other mobility assistance equipment that may be necessary.

While they should be able to pack their own bug-out bag, they may need a detailed checklist to follow to ensure they don't leave anything out. You know your loved one and what level of support they'll need for this. If, however, they live in a nursing home, you will probably need to do more for them. Make sure you have a bug-out bag prepared for them and a plan for how you will carry it if they're unable to. Make sure you have copies of their medical needs and all the supplies you need to cater to them.

BUGGING OUT WITH SOMEONE WITH A HEALTH CONDITION

The main thing here is to know what you're dealing with. You need to know the health condition and what treatments it needs in order to continue those treatments for as long as possible in the case of an emergency. Of course, not every condition is treatable, and in these cases, you'll need to know how to manage the situation and what you can do to help your loved one survive a disaster until medical assistance is available. If possible, look for treatments that don't rely on electricity and that you can fall back on if the worst happens. The goal is to avoid a sharp decline in health if you find yourself suddenly without power or cut off from your usual treatment options. This can pose a problem when it comes to stockpiling medication, as there are laws and regulations that make it difficult to stock up. Some mail-order prescription services will deliver 90 days' worth of medication in one go, and this is worth considering if your loved one's medication isn't subject to regular change. It's also worth looking into alternative medications that will help some symptoms in a pinch, including vitamins and supplements to support their overall health.

Diet plays a considerable role in our health, and this is even more pronounced when a medical condition is in play. Make sure your loved one knows which foods aggravate and alleviate their symptoms, and plan for this in your supply inventory.

BUGGING OUT WITH ANIMALS

The first thing to consider is whether your pet is capable of bugging out. For some animals, it may be kinder to leave plenty of food and water out and leave them at home. Certainly, smaller pets like rodents, fish, and rabbits will make your journey much more difficult, and they will rely on you for everything. In some cases, it may be appropriate to take your cat, but you will need to carry them the whole way, and it may be difficult to keep track of them once you reach your location.

Dogs are the pets most compatible with a bug-out situation, and for many, coming with you will be appropriate. I'm confident that my three are well-prepared and could come with us, but if their health deteriorates, I know we'll have to reassess the situation. Weigh the pros and cons before you make your decision. On the plus side, they provide valuable companionship and add to the group's warmth and security. On the downside, they are an extra mouth to feed and mean you need extra supplies. They are an extra responsibility, and they may struggle to keep up with the pace. Unless you can train them not to bark when it's not necessary, they can also be as much of a danger as they are a security asset, potentially giving away your location. You know your dog: Think carefully about whether they're capable of bugging out. Take into account their age, their health, and the conditions they will need to navigate.

If you decide to take your dog with you, you'll need to train them. Gradually increase the length of their daily walk (the bonus here is that you'll be training yourself, too!) and get them used to wearing a saddlebag. Start with an empty pack, gradually upping the weight until they're used to carrying everything they'll need to. Take them on overnight camping trips to get them used to various conditions, and make sure they're well-trained both on and off the leash.

The Doggy Bug-Out Bag

Food: Your dog will need extra calories in a survival situation, particularly if you'll be walking intensely. They may need between 50% and 100% more calories. Rather than canned food, go for freeze-dried kibble, which packs a lot of calories in a smaller amount of weight. Some dog energy bars would also be a good idea for when a quick burst of energy would be useful.

Water: To determine how much water your dog will need, divide their weight by eight. The result is the number of cups of water they'll need daily.

First aid: Having been on one myself, I'd recommend taking a first aid course for dogs. Many of the things you have in your first aid kit will also work for your dog, but you will need a few extras too. You'll need their monthly flea and tick treatment, a supply of Sulfadene or another canine skin ointment, hydrogen peroxide for cleaning wounds, Metronidazole (for treating waterborne diseases), electrolyte powders (in case of dehydration), and an antibiotic ointment and gauze.

Clothing: This is breed-dependent, but you may need raincoats and sweaters if you have a less hardy dog. Dog booties are a good idea for all dogs. Rough terrain can be tough on paws, and these will help protect them and keep them injury-free. Remember that you'll need to get your dog used to wearing these first.

★ TAKE ACTION!

Doggy BOB Checklist

Use this checklist to make sure your dog is bug-out ready. Remember that you will need to train them to carry a pack before they can do this reliably. I have added a few extra items that didn't fit into the main categories. You know your dog's needs, and if you think something isn't appropriate for them, feel free to leave it off your list.

- collapsible bowl
- collar with ID and vaccination evidence
- dog booties
- dog food

- extra water
- favorite toy
- first aid kit
- muzzle (if appropriate)
- paw wax
- raincoat/jacket/sweater as appropriate
- reflective dog jacket
- secure leash
- sleeping mat
- towel
- well-fitting saddlebag (with waterproof cover)

You have your location, your route, and your transport all set. You have as much as you can carry in your bug-out bag, and you know your location is as well-prepared for all members of your group as possible. But you need one more thing in your arsenal: a survival cache located somewhere on your route. This is what we'll look at in the next chapter.

8

TREASURES ON THE ROAD: PREPARE YOUR SURVIVAL CACHE

I don't know how many times I used the expression, "Don't put all your eggs in one basket," before its meaning truly hit home. We were on vacation once, and we stopped at a diner for something to eat on the way. The parking lot was full, and we parked a little way down the road, knowing nothing of the neighborhood or how safe the car would be. Honestly, I didn't think twice about it. We returned to pick up the car, revived and ready for the next leg of the journey, only to find it missing, along with everything we needed for our trip. I had put all my eggs in one basket, and that basket had been stolen. I tell you this story because it was an important lesson in survival planning, and that eggs-in-a-basket expression is important when you're thinking about your bug-out bag. Your bag is your basket, and your supplies are your eggs—lose your bag, and you lose all your supplies too. That's why you need a backup plan, and that backup plan is your survival cache.

WHAT IS A SURVIVAL CACHE?

In simple terms, a survival cache is a secret hiding place for survival supplies. It gives you an alternative way of accessing emergency supplies if something goes wrong. That could be that you're away from home when disaster strikes and you don't have your bug-out bag or access to the supplies you have at home, or it could be that your bag is lost, stolen, or damaged while you're on the move. A survival cache can also be used as a restocking point along the way to your location, allowing you to carry a lighter load. And you can have more than one; in that case, it can be used to spread your gear out in different locations en route to your final destination.

WHAT SHOULD YOUR SURVIVAL CACHE CONTAIN?

The contents of your survival cache will be similar to those of your bug-out bag, but there are a few ways in which they will differ. For a start, I'd recommend keeping the less expensive versions of an item in the cache—keep your good knife for your bag, for example, and put the cheaper version in the cache. If the sole purpose of your cache is a backup to your bug-out bag, you don't need to think much beyond this. However, if you have several caches in place and plan to use them for different purposes, you'll have to think more carefully, and this is the approach I'd recommend.

To illustrate this, let's consider a scenario in which your bug-out location is 50 miles away, and you need to get there on foot. Your cache at the 10-mile mark may contain extra rations of water, a fresh set of clothes, and a tent—everything you need for the first night of the journey. At the halfway point, you might stash extra food, water, and your fishing kit. Consider the number of caches you want and how you plan to use them before you decide exactly what they should contain.

What we'll look at here is a broad overview of what you might need to store in your cache, but plan carefully for your own route, location, and the number of stashes. That said, some basic supplies should be included in any cache you have, no matter how many there are or what else you plan to store in them:

- batteries
- clothes
- emergency blanket
- firestarter/matches
- first aid kit
- flashlight
- food
- knife
- rope

- tarp
- tent
- water

As you know, I tend to steer clear of firearms, but if you're using them, spare ammunition is something you'll want to store in some of your caches. I'm assuming you've packed water filters in your bug-out bag, and if you have several, you may not feel the need for a backup. However, since they don't take up much room, an emergency stash is always a good idea, and I'd include an extra one in your cache. Although you already have a flashlight and batteries on your list, a few candles as an emergency fallback plan wouldn't go amiss. A multi-tool, a fishing kit, a backup communication device, and copies of your maps are also good ideas. You'll probably want to add some essential hygiene items, and if you have the space, you could even include one or two things you could use for bartering if necessary. This might be some extra first aid supplies or some alcohol—things that could become precious resources in an emergency.

THE CONTAINER

Choosing the right container for your cache is more important than you might realize. Get it wrong, and your supplies can easily deteriorate. The best container for you will depend on the environment in which you'll be stashing it, but wood is a bad choice in most cases. Wood rots easily, and this puts your supplies in jeopardy.

Your main enemy will be moisture, so in most cases, the best containers will be made of either plastic or metal. Although metal is likely to rust over a long period of time, it does have the advantage of keeping pests out, and rust isn't a problem if you're placing it in a low-moisture environment. If you'll be hiding your cache in moist soil, however, your best bet is a plastic container with a waterproof seal. Rodents are a risk in this case, as they're capable of gnawing through plastic, and that will make the watertight seal redundant. Weigh the pros of cons of each within the environment you'll be storing it in before you make your decision. Whatever you decide on, I'd recommend placing all your supplies in zip-top bags with oxygen absorbers for extra protection.

I've tried and tested a few different containers over the years, and having weeded out the least successful, these are my suggestions:

PVC Pipe

A PVC pipe container has several size options and is a nice affordable choice. They're great if you want to store your cache underground, as they're watertight and easy to bury. And the chances are, if someone comes across them, they'll just think they're pieces of pipe and won't be inspired to loot. To be on the safe side, use a strong sealant to make sure it's completely waterproof.

To secure a cap to the end of your pipe, simply use PVC cement. Word to the wise though: If you do this to both ends, you'll need something to cut the tube open, or you won't be able to access your store. Trust me: I've made this mistake on a trial run. Instead, you can insert a rubber gasket into the other end. As you tighten its wing nut, the rubber will be pushed to the inside of the tube, creating a seal. You can then add a cap to close the pipe. In the Take Action section at the end of this chapter, we'll run through exactly how to make a PVC pipe container.

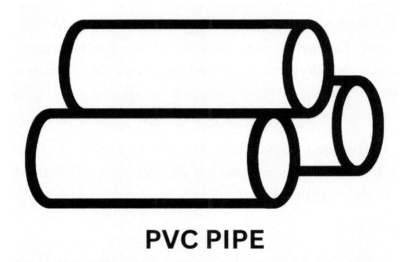

PVC PIPE

Ammo Can

Ammo cans are a good option for dry climates like the desert. As they're made of metal, they're less suitable for a high-moisture environment as rust is a risk. Most come with a waterproof seal, but they're still prone to rust and corrosion, so unless you live somewhere dry, they're better as a short-term option.

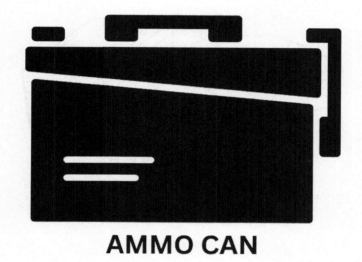

AMMO CAN

Metal/Plastic Storage Container

Your local hardware store will stock a range of metal and plastic storage containers. They're well built, weather resistant, and come in many different sizes. Again, you'll need to add a strong sealant to ensure they're waterproof. You could also look into waterproof boxes, which shouldn't require any extra sealant. Remember that larger containers will be harder to bury, so keep your container as small as possible for what you intend to store.

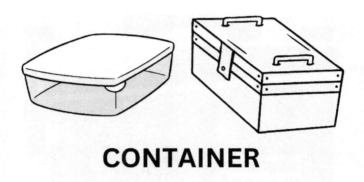

CONTAINER

Metal/Plastic Trash Can

These are a great option, but you'll need to be more careful with sealant as trash cans aren't designed to be waterproof. Don't be tempted to go for large cans. While the storage space may be appealing, they're far less convenient. A medium-sized or small trash can will suffice.

TRASH CAN

THE ADVANTAGE OF HAVING MULTIPLE CACHES

Having more survival caches only means being better prepared. You'll be able to restock more easily if you need to, and the more of them you have, the less need for them to be large. You can't really have too many; you just have to make sure you know what's in them so you know where to go for what you need. This may not be so easy when they're spread out along your route. You need to think about what you'll need for each stage of your journey, but if you have them spread out around your bug-out location, you'll have a backup if you start to run out of supplies. Returning to the proverb we began the chapter with, the more baskets you can spread your eggs among, the less likely you are to lose everything if one disaster happens. If you do have a lot of caches, though, I'd suggest marking them all on your map so that you don't forget where you've hidden them. We'll look more closely at ways to remember where your caches are further down the chapter.

THE BEST LOCATIONS FOR A SURVIVAL CACHE

The key to choosing the best place to hide your cache lies in remembering what it's there for. It's there to fall back on if your bug-out bag is compromised or you can't get to it for some reason; it's there to allow you to restock your supplies; and it's there to provide you with what you need en route to your destination. With all these factors in mind, deciding where to place your cache should reveal itself to you naturally.

You'll want to hide it on the route to your bug-out location (and remember, that will mean having one on each of your routes), somewhere secluded but easy for you to reach. You may also want to place them around your bug-out location so you can restock easily or for peace of mind that you'll still have supplies if your hideout gets looted. I'd also recommend hiding an extra one in your home. That way, if bugging in is the more appropriate course of action but your home is looted, you'll still have some supplies on hand. Personally, I have a network of caches spread out everywhere—my home and my bug-out location, with alternative stashes on each route.

Any hiding place you use should be well away from where you live, ideally in a remote area that you can access easily but where you'll be unseen when hiding or retrieving your supplies. The best way to choose those hiding places is by process of elimination: There are certain places where hiding a cache would be a bad idea. I've heard many tales of people hiding caches in abandoned buildings, but this isn't wise. In an emergency, these places may be used as refuges, and if that happens, you won't be able to access your cache discreetly. They also often get burned down, meaning you wouldn't have a stash to fall back on at all. Commercial storage units aren't a sensible choice either, as they'd be prime targets in a crisis, and if you suspect that a location might be used for development, you'll want to avoid that too. If there's any chance your cache could be destroyed or discovered during construction work, it's not a good hiding place.

You also want to avoid flood zones, which, if your cache hadn't already been destroyed by flooding, it might be dangerous to retrieve it. You should also steer clear of a main road or escape route; you want it to be hidden from sight and possible to retrieve discreetly.

CHOOSING A HIDING PLACE

The first decision you must make is whether to hide your cache in a natural location or use an existing structure. Natural hiding spots are entirely dependent on your environment and could include fallen trees or shrubs, river banks, or caves. In these cases, your natural environment is what you trust to keep the cache hidden. Your other option is to hide it within an existing structure, although, as we've discussed, many of these (such as abandoned buildings) aren't wise choices. However, a few structures could work for you. Perhaps you have a shed on an allotment along your route, or maybe you have a mobile home you could stash it under.

There's some debate about the best way to hide a cache, but most agree that burying it is a solid option. If you take this route, you want to bury it somewhere that you can access easily, and you want to bury it deep enough that it remains hidden but not so deep that digging it up is a major project. Make sure the top of your cache is a few feet below ground level, and take note of the natural markers in the area so that you know exactly where it is.

You're not a squirrel, though, and for most of us, even a natural marker won't help us remember exactly where we buried our treasure, so make sure you mark the location on your map.

Burying a cache isn't a guaranteed way to protect it, and water damage is a risk. You can guard against this to some extent by not burying it too deep and making sure your container is watertight. Remember that a natural land-mark may not be there forever—logs and rocks can be moved, and even trees can be taken down, so make sure you have a few ways of identifying where you buried your cache. Ensure your map is detailed enough to find it even if all your landmarks disappear. Use GPS coordinates and count paces from a road, for example, to the exact spot where you buried your cache.

Just as you need to rotate your supplies, you'll need to check in on your cache even after it's been buried. You should dig it up at least once a year to make sure it's still there and that your supplies are still in good condition. It would also be wise to stay on top of local news to make sure there's no development being planned near your hiding place. As soon as you hear of something like this in the works, you know it's time to move your cache.

Another option is to submerge your container in shallow water, but if you do this, you'll need to be absolutely sure that it's 100% watertight. If you live near a pond, river, or stream, burying it on the bank might be an option, or you could submerge it further out. If you do this, however, you'll need a way to retrieve it—most likely a rope and a float and access to it by boat. This is a risky option, but if it's plausible for you, it does make your cache far less likely to be discovered by someone else.

PROTECTING AND FINDING YOUR CACHE

Once your cache is out in the wild, there's only so much you can do to protect it. Most of the protection comes in the hiding stage—the better hidden it is, the more protected it is. When considering your hiding place, factor in who might be traveling past and why they might be there. If you know, for example, that metal detectorists tend to visit a particular area, you know that this won't be a good place to hide your cache. Once your cache is hidden, checking it regularly and rotating your supplies will keep you informed if something has gone awry and allow you to make sure everything is in the best condition possible.

We've discussed using natural markers and maps to make sure you can find your cache again; to be sure you can track it down quickly, I'd recommend having a distinct map purely to find your cache. Ideally, that map will be drawn so that only you and your family can read it. This will protect the secrecy of your hiding place. It may sound a bit over the top, but the strategy I've taken for this is drawing my map on two pieces of tracing paper, with only half the map on each one. The only way the map is complete is when those pieces of paper are placed over top of each other. I keep both sheets in different places, and I'm confident that if someone were to find one, they wouldn't be able to understand the full picture of the map. You could also use GPS tracking, although you'll need a high-quality tracker and rechargeable batteries for this.

The last thing to note about finding your cache is that it's crucial that anyone in your family can find it. You don't want someone who's stumbled upon your map accidentally to be able to read it, but you do want to be sure that if your family became separated, any one of you would be able to access your emergency supplies if necessary.

★ TAKE ACTION!

DIY PVC Pipe Survival Cache

I'm a big fan of the PVC pipe as a survival cache, and I have several of these stashed along each alternative route to my bug-out location. We've touched on them a little already, but a quick tutorial will set you on the road if you've never made one. Have a go, and you'll soon be convinced.

What You'll Need:

- PVC pipe (any diameter you choose)
- 2x PVC caps
- 1 test plug
- PVC cement
- saw (if you need to cut the pipe to length)
- silica gel
- thin sock

Method:

1. Cut PVC to your desired length if necessary.
2. Attach a cap to one end of the pipe using PVC cement.
3. Allow the cement to cure fully.
4. Pour silica gel into a clean sock, secure it with a knot, and place this in the pipe.
5. Add your supplies to the pipe.
6. Insert the test plug into the open end of the pipe and tighten it.

Now, with your home, your bug-out location, and everything you need to get you there safely in place, it's time to start thinking about securing your bases, and that's what we'll come to in the next chapter.

9

SECURING YOUR BASES ... BOTH
AT HOME AND ON THE ROAD

Did you ever play Capture the Flag as a kid? Bear with me ... It's more relevant than it sounds! The goal is for each team to capture an opposing team's flag and take it back to their territory. The thing is, it isn't just about capturing the flag—you also have to protect your own flag and avoid capture on the way back to your territory. You want to keep and protect your flag from everyone else who wants it—because it's in everyone's best interest to have that flag in their territory. This is comparable to the value of your bug-out location —you're not the only one who wants a safe and well-equipped place to shelter, and in an emergency situation, you may face some rivalry. In this chapter, we'll look at how you can protect against that rivalry, as well as skills you can learn to keep yourself safe when you're in transit.

As we discussed in Chapter Six, a large part of making sure your bug-out location is secure relates to choosing the right spot in the first place. It should be in a secluded area with plenty of tree cover, ideally with a natural barrier like a river or a mountain to make it more difficult for others to reach. You can use this natural camouflage to its best possible advantage by also making sure there are strategic places that will allow you to keep an eye out for potential threats. You should also be aware of your location's strengths and weaknesses, utilizing that knowledge as well as you can to keep a closer eye on weaker spots and spend less time on areas that are naturally more secure. Getting these fundamental components right in the early stages will go a long way toward keeping your location safe, but there are a few extra precautions you can take to increase your security.

ADDITIONAL SECURITY PRECAUTIONS

As you know by now, I see being prepared as a never-ending journey. There's always more you can do to prepare both your home and your bug-out location for an emergency, and these additional precautions are all details you can work on or add to over the years. As long as your site is in a good, secluded spot and you're confident that it won't be an immediate target for rivals, you can focus on stocking up and preparing your supplies first so that you know you'll have everything you need if disaster strikes.

All these additional security elements can be added as you go along.

Cameras

The best security cameras run on batteries and are equipped with motion sensors. These will let you know if someone is on your property, allow you to see what's going on, and give you something to look back on if you require proof of an intrusion later on. The advantage of seeing what's going on if someone stumbles onto your property is that you have time to take precautions rather than being caught unawares. Those extra few minutes may seem small, but they're enough to allow you a hasty exit if necessary. I'd advise against fake cameras designed simply to scare away intruders. These may work for protecting your house against burglars under ordinary circumstances, but they're unlikely to deter someone in desperate circumstances. You could, however, use game cameras if you're using your location regularly (for example, if it's also a hunting lodge). These are easy to transport and can be set up anywhere you choose.

Motion Sensor Floodlights

Motion sensor floodlights are available in solar models, and I'd highly recommend these for your bug-out location. They'll deter unwelcome animals and people, and they can be carried with you or stored inside and set up when you need them. Not only will they deter trespassers, but they'll also alert you to their presence after daylight hours, giving you time to take precautions.

Thorny Bushes

Ideally, your bug-out location already has plenty of tree coverage, but you can add to this by planting thorny bushes like roses and cacti (depending on where you live). These will make it more difficult for intruders to make their way onto your property and keep animals at bay. Bear in mind that planting any kind of bush is a long-term plan, however, as they take time to grow. You'll want to do this as soon as you can, and it may only be possible if you own your property and the land it sits on.

Electric Shock Fences and Boobie Traps

The chances are that an electric shock fence labeled as such will be enough to send out a clear message that strangers are unwelcome without anyone needing to get hurt. That said, electric shock fences deliver minimal shocks, and no one will be seriously harmed if they touch one. You can also use boobie traps, increasing in intensity as they get closer to your property. I would advise, however, that you use these cautiously, particularly if you have children or vulnerable people with you. I personally try to avoid using boobie traps because of the risk to my own children.

In a similar vein but less harmful, however, are DIY alarms, which you can place at the entry points to your property to warn you if someone is approaching. We'll look at how to make a mousetrap-tripwire alarm in our Take Action section at the end of the chapter.

Your Relationship With the Community

It may not sound like much of a defense strategy, but your relationship with the community is important. Your location should be secluded, but that doesn't necessarily mean that there will be no one in the vicinity. Get to know anyone who lives there and make an effort to get to know the area and the crime rates in the nearest neighborhood. All of this gives you useful data points and tells you a certain amount about your potential security in times of crisis. Getting to know the neighbors, meanwhile, means there are more of you to look out for each other in an emergency situation.

Safety in Numbers

There's safety in numbers, and while a bigger group may draw more attention, it's also more likely to be able to protect itself in the event of an attack. This is something you'll want to consider in your overall bug-out plan. Will it just be you and your immediate family, or will you pair up with another family or include some friends? If you have more people on your team, you can also afford to employ extra security measures like having someone on sentry duty patrol the property and alert the rest of the group to danger. A dog can also be a good asset here, but remember that unwanted barking may draw attention.

Being Wise About Valuables

While you do want your bug-out location to be adequately stocked and ready to move into at a moment's notice, I'd advise against leaving anything valuable there. Important personal documents should be kept on your person. If you would like to store valuable things away from home, a well-hidden survival cache is a better idea than keeping them at your bug-out location.

BEYOND PHYSICAL PRECAUTIONS

While making sure your bug-out location is as secure as possible is important, a good security plan goes beyond any of the physical precautions you can take. We live in a world where our personal data is everywhere, and protecting it in an emergency is just as important as protecting our physical possessions. As with any preparations, this should be done well in advance of an emergency because, chances are, a computer virus or worm is likely to hit you before any physical disaster does. Make sure you have a copy of essential documents like your birth certificates, social security cards, recent pictures of each family member, and all your contact information. Ideally, that data should be stored in several locations, including an external hard drive that you can carry with you.

It would be wise to back up additional data too—things like world knowledge and online encyclopedias. That way, if the internet goes down, you still have access to some of the information that would have been available to you under normal circumstances. You could even keep copies of novels that are out of their copyright period. Project Gutenberg is a good place to go for this. If an emergency goes on for a long time and life as we know it completely changes, that reading material could be a real sanity saver.

SECURING YOURSELF AND YOUR FAMILY

Ultimately, any security measures you put in place are working toward the same goal: protecting you and your family. To do this effectively, you'll also need to be streetwise and know how to defend yourself if danger approaches. I've broken this down into three key areas to think about.

Situational Awareness

Situational awareness simply means being aware of the world around you, which is something to train yourself in well before any emergency. Try not to walk around with your nose in your phone. Pay attention to your environment and the people around you. Looking alert is a surprisingly effective way to protect yourself. Someone buried in their phone and not paying attention to who's nearby is far more likely to get mugged than someone looking at their environment. While you don't want to be paranoid about every little thing, it's important to pay attention to any potential danger so that you can react when you need to, and this will serve you well in a crisis situation. You can train your kids to do this by asking them questions about their environment or giving them particular things to look out for—like an on-the-go version of Eye Spy.

Blending In

In a survival situation, the last thing you want to do is stand out. For example, you don't want to be remembered for buying large amounts of food or supplies. Do what you can to minimize this risk, avoiding particularly remarkable outfits that draw attention. Wear neutral tones and avoid bright colors that will attract attention. Blending in is an extension of situational awareness; pay attention to those around you and match your behavior to theirs so that you don't stand out. This is also a great game you can play with your kids, and it's super useful as a child-taming strategy when they're being a bit wild! Get them to pay attention to the people around them and act as if they are one of them. My kids can play this game for hours, and they're getting very good at it.

Self Defense

Again, I'd like to leave firearms out of this discussion, but if you live in an area where you're allowed to carry a weapon, this may be something you want to consider. If you do this, however, be sure to get proper training and follow the appropriate licensing procedures. Whether or not you have firearms, learning how to defend yourself without one is a must. I'd recommend martial arts classes for this; again, this is something everyone in the family can get involved in. Martial arts classes prepare you well in a number of ways. Not only do you learn how to defend yourself, but you also learn how to fall well, thus avoiding injury and building your self-confidence, which can deter potential attackers on its own.

Martial arts is a very broad umbrella, and there are many you can choose from. We touched on this in Chapter Four, and you may remember that my particular recommendations were muay Thai, boxing, and jiu-jitsu. There are a few other defensive styles you may wish to look into as well, one being krav maga, which was developed by the Israeli Defense Forces. It is perfect for quickly disabling an attacker and combines well-known arts like boxing, judo, and jujitsu with real-life situations you might encounter.

Of course, any martial art you learn is determined, to some extent, by what's available in your area. Read reviews and make sure you find a reputable instructor before you commit to a class. My whole family is currently learning judo, all at age-appropriate levels. This is part of our long-term training plan, and the kids love it.

★ TAKE ACTION!

Make a Mousetrap Trip Wire

A mousetrap isn't just good for catching mice. It's also a good starting point for a tripwire alarm. I prefer this kind of DIY project to a boobie trap, but if you have children, be mindful of where you place it. Although it won't cause any harm to an intruder and simply works to alert you of a threat, it could be a hazard to a small child or elderly person. Place it wisely, and make sure everyone in your party knows about it.

What You'll Need:

- a mousetrap
- wire cutters
- ring caps
- fishing line
- zip ties

Method:

1. Remove the holding bar from the nail on the mousetrap, carefully leaving the loop intact.
2. Use wire cutters to trim the bar behind the arch so that you're left with a straight bar.

3. Remove the bait holder catch.

4. Pull the hammer back a couple of times, allowing it to spring back and mark the wood to show you the contact points.

5. Remove the arm of the spring from the hammer and turn the hammer to the side.

6. At each of the contact points, add a small nail, leaving the head slightly raised from the wood.

7. Turn the hammer back to its original position and reattach the spring.

8. Pull back the hammer, and slide the holding bar through the U-shaped nail to hold it in place.

9. Place a ring cap on each nail.

10. Tie a knot in a piece of fishing line, creating a loop that you can slide onto the holding bar.

11. Put your tripwire in place by tying the other end of the fishing wire to something strong and secure, and mount the trap using zip ties.

12. Your tripwire is alarmed and ready! If someone's foot touches the fishing line, the bar will be pulled, and the alarm will sound.

Although it's important that your bug-out location is secure, it's also important to make sure the home you're leaving behind is safe. You can learn more about this in my earlier book, *When Crisis Hits Suburbia*, but remember that all of the precautions we've discussed in this chapter can also be applied to your home.

You now know everything you need to bug out effectively in an emergency, which leaves us with one final piece of the puzzle. In the next chapter, we'll look at how to plan your exit—without cutting yourself off in the process.

10

MAKE A SWIFT EXIT WITHOUT CUTTING YOURSELF OFF: PLANNING AND COMMUNICATION

The very first time I did a test run to my bug-out location, I discovered that I'd overlooked an essential part of the plan: I hadn't covered my route out of the city thoroughly enough. As soon as I hit heavy traffic, I realized that if there was an emergency and everyone was trying to flee, this would be a problem. I instantly knew my plan needed work. The first thing I'd have to do to correct the problem would be to make a proper exit plan—with backups. We discussed this in Chapter Five, but now we need to take it a step further. Planning your exit isn't just about planning how you'll get to your location; it's planning the whole evacuation from the moment you make the call to leave to the moment you arrive at your bug-out spot.

PRE-PLANNING

It's a strange way to put it (after all, planning *is* preplanning—being prepared in advance), but I find this a helpful way to think about the planning process. When I talk about pre-planning, I'm really talking about everything we've covered so far—training yourself and your family, organizing your bug-out bag, and preparing your location. Self-awareness is a key component of ensuring all of this works for you. Knowing what you're good at already and what you need to work on will help you know where you still need to train. After all, preparing your location and supplies is useless if you don't know what to do with anything you've prepared. Making sure you have the right mindset is also important; it's amazing how much more you can accomplish when you believe in your abilities, and a positive attitude goes a long way in lifting everyone else up and motivating them too.

A certain amount of forward-thinking and hypothesizing is helpful as well. Consider what disasters are likely in the area you live in. That means learning about the area's history and knowing what natural disasters have happened there in the past. Have there been floods, for example, or is it in an earthquake zone? Factoring these details into your plan makes it much easier to develop a concrete strategy, as you can eliminate some options from the outset. The same concept can be applied to what you've already ascertained about your strengths and weaknesses. Taking these into account not only helps you direct your training in the most beneficial way, but it also means you can tailor your plan to use your strengths to their best advantage. If, for example, you know your fitness is good, you may be able to plan for a longer route or to carry more supplies. Your weaknesses, meanwhile, will tell you what you need to study and practice.

One important calculation you'll need to make has to do with your travel speed. If you're able to calculate the rate at which you travel, you can work out how long it will realistically take you to reach your bug-out location, and in turn, this will help you plan for the number of supplies you'll need to carry or cache. Remember that this isn't as simple as calculating your walking or cycling speed under ordinary circumstances. You'll need to factor in the weight of your bug-out bag and the terrain you'll have to navigate. This is why trial runs are so important. You'll need to have a good idea of what you can carry and how the landscape will affect your speed, and you'll need to adjust your plans to accommodate what you discover. Of course, you're not the only person to consider in this equation, and once you've tried out the route yourself, you'll need to do it with the whole family and make adjustments accordingly. I know I had to shift my own plans somewhat when I realized my youngest son was struggling to keep up with the weight of his bag.

FINALIZING AN EXIT PLAN

You can plan your escape routes to a certain extent, but ultimately, they'll be determined by what happens in the specific emergency. This means you'll need options, which you'll need to work out with your whole family. When I did this, I bribed them with cake and insisted we all sat around the kitchen table with a map. Your goal is to come up with meeting points that everybody is familiar with, and you'll need several points in each cardinal direction. I'd recommend having a minimum of three possibilities in each direction: one close to home, one on the city's outskirts, and one outside it. If your family isn't familiar with any of them and you can't find options they do know, make sure to visit each one so they're all clear on where you should meet.

Think of route planning as a long-term project. This isn't necessarily something that can be done effectively in one afternoon. Practice going to work by as many different routes as possible, getting to know the secrets of your city. You'll learn a lot about the different options available to you that way, and you'll pick up important details about the landscape that you probably weren't aware of. Aim for lesser-known paths for each of your routes, and factor in traffic at the busiest times of the day—these are likely to be reflective of the congestion levels in an emergency.

KEY QUESTIONS TO ASK YOURSELF

How effective your evacuation will be is determined by the timing and efficiency with which it's executed. You're unlikely to have much warning when a crisis hits, and your response will be dictated by the circumstances at the time. The best way to deal with this is to nurture a crisis mindset, which starts with remaining calm under pressure. From there, there are eight key questions you can ask yourself that will help you assess whether it's time to bug out and how you will do so effectively. If you're not convinced you'll remember these questions in an emergency, copy them and keep them with your emergency plan.

1. Is everyone OK?
2. Exactly what has happened?
3. Is it safe to remain at home?
4. If we need to evacuate, how quickly do we need to move?
5. Which direction is the wind blowing in? (Be aware of airborne dangers.)
6. What supplies do I have with me?
7. What are the weather conditions?
8. Which direction should I move in (based on the specific emergency)?

COMMUNICATION PLANNING

If the circumstances require you to bug out, it's likely that the environment is changing rapidly, and that means you'll need up-to-date information in order to stay safe. This makes communication extremely important, both for the purposes of accessing information and staying in contact with your loved ones. A successful exit strategy requires you not only to leave safely but also to avoid cutting yourself off in the process.

The first thing to ensure is that you have a physical copy of all the contact details for your friends and family, as well as emergency numbers and the contact information for official government agencies. These will help you to stay in contact and access updates about the emergency.

It's likely that mobile phone networks will go down fairly quickly in a disaster, but you may be lucky for a few hours. If that happens, you'll be able to initiate your evacuation plan with messages, but it's unwise to rely solely on this strategy. Walkie-talkies are a good backup plan for communicating within the group, but getting information from the wider world is also important, and you have a few options here. All of these options are discussed in more detail in my previous book, *Prepare Your Home for a Sudden Grid-Down Situation*, but we'll cover them briefly here. Bear in mind that there are also other signaling options for when you need to catch someone's attention or send a message silently. These include mirrors, lights, and glow sticks, and these will be essential for some of the subtle communication strategies we'll look at shortly.

Hand Crank Radio

A hand crank radio will allow you to tap into radio waves, even over some distance, particularly AM frequencies., and this will be extremely useful for getting weather updates. This is especially important when escaping a weather-related emergency like a hurricane or a wildfire. If you don't already have a hand crank radio, I'd suggest getting one with solar capabilities that comes with a flashlight, a phone charger, and NOAA weather.

Ham Radio

Ham radio is extremely effective for long-distance communication, and there are plenty of handheld devices you can use without needing to set up a huge station. You can easily keep your costs down to under $200, but this will only be worth it if you know how to use it. It can be a steep learning curve if you're a beginner, and I'd recommend going on a course if you seriously intend to use it. Bear in mind that you will also need a Federal Communications Commission (FCC) license to operate ham radio legally.

CB Radio

Because it doesn't require you to pass a licensing exam and it's nowhere near as challenging to learn as ham radio, a CB radio is a more realistic option for most people. You can't transmit over as long of distances as you can with ham radio, but in a bug-out scenario, its reach will probably be sufficient. You can get both vehicle units and handheld models, so you can pick what best suits your plan. I'd recommend Cobra as a starting point when you're researching brands.

Walkie-Talkies

Walkie-talkies are simple yet very useful in a bug-out situation. If someone in your group has to leave your location for supplies, walkie-talkies allow you to stay in touch. Also, if someone is away from the shelter and has an accident or encounters danger, they can call for help. Again, you can get vehicle units or handheld models, and they're great to have as a backup, even if you also have a radio for accessing information about the local environment.

Satellite Phone

Satellite phones are expensive, and there's always the risk that your calls could be intercepted. However, they do work well even when cell phone service is unavailable—unless the satellites go down. If you don't have a device that also allows voice communication, you're limited to very short messages, so you'll need to be well-practiced at this. I'd recommend the Garmin Inreach Explorer if you're interested in a satellite phone—this is what I have, and it's served me well on campsites where there's been no cell phone signal.

Communication Strategies

Once you've settled on your equipment, you'll need to think about how you will convey any message you need to send more subtly.

Morse code is one option and would be extremely useful if you needed to communicate with someone in an adjacent room (you could do this by tapping the code on the wall) or across a long distance (which could be done using a flashlight). It requires time to learn, but it would be a fun family project; I can attest to this because we've spent many Sunday afternoons working on it in my family. My boys love it. You could also learn how to send messages using flags, which might be particularly useful if you're planning to use a boat. Again, this will require practice and relies on good visibility. Military hand signals can also be used to quietly convey information, or you can devise your own set of signals for your family. Just be sure that everyone is consistent and knows exactly what each one means. I haven't done this with my family, but I have to say, I do like the idea. No one from outside the group will be able to tell what you're saying, no matter what their training.

★ TAKE ACTION!

Make Your Bug-Out Plan

Every family's bug-out plan will be unique, and there will always be certain elements dictated by the specifics of the emergency. However, to get you started, I've created a template based on my evacuation strategy. Create your own or fill in this one, adapting it to your own needs as you go along. Some sections include an example to give further guidance.

Section 1: Group Members

Name	Phone Number	Special Needs	Skills
Jack	333-333-3333	Nut allergy	Map reading

Section 2: Assembly Points

Assembly Point	Location Name	Specific Location	Exit Point
Primary	Home	Hallway	Front door
Alternative 1			
Alternative 2			
Alternative 3			

Section 3: Bug-Out Locations

Name of Location	Directions	Waypoints	Location of Supply Caches
Primary location	Route 1:		
	Route 2:		
	Route 3:		
Alternative 1	Route 1:		
	Route 2:		
	Route 3:		
Alternative 2	Route 1:		
	Route 2:		
	Route 3:		

Section 4: Emergency Contacts

Incorporate the Family Evacuation Plan you made in Chapter Five here so that you have all of your emergency contacts included in your plan.

Following the advice in every chapter up until this point gives you the backbone of this plan, but you need to make sure you tie it all together and know exactly what you're going to do if the worst happens. This is the final piece of the puzzle, and as you work through your trial runs, you can refine it and make sure it's watertight and ready to see you through any emergency.

PREPARATION FOR ALL

It's never too late to prepare... until it is. As you start putting your bug-out plan together, it's natural that you may start to worry about those who are less well prepared for an emergency. You can help point other people in the right direction simply by leaving a review.

By sharing your honest opinion of this book on Amazon, you'll show new readers where they can find all the information they need to make sure their families are fully prepared for the worst.

WANT TO HELP OTHERS?

Thank you so much for your support. The more people have access to the resources they need to prepare, the more people will stay strong, healthy and safe, no matter what happens.

Scan the QR code below to leave your review:

CONCLUSION

You can never be completely prepared for a disaster. Nothing can prepare you for how you may feel the moment an emergency strikes, and there's no way of predicting the way every single detail will pan out. But what you can do is make sure you're prepared to hunker down at home or bug out when necessary, and you now have all the information you need to make a solid bug-out plan. You know what to pack and how to make sure your family is as prepared as possible, and you know how to tell the difference between an emergency that requires you to shelter in place and one that means you must evacuate. Never stop learning; never stop refining, and your plan will begin to emerge piece by piece.

Trial runs will be key to ensuring your bug-out plan is successful, and you may find that your first run leaves you in a state of mild panic. Don't worry—this is exactly what trial runs are for. Keep a determined and focused mindset, and work on those areas of your plan that showed up as lacking. I've done many trial runs for my bug-out plan, testing each route multiple times, and I can tell you I encountered some steep learning curves in the beginning. But as I honed my plan, I found more and more success with each run, and I'm absolutely confident that my family will know exactly what to do if the worst happens. Every hole you discover in your plan is a learning opportunity. Don't let it dishearten you. Instead, be thankful that you found out well in advance of any emergency and had the opportunity to correct the mistake.

You can reach this same level of confidence. Follow the advice in each chapter of the book, working through methodically and building your plan piece by piece. That dedication and commitment are all you need to make sure you have a solid bug-out plan to see you through any emergency that requires you to evacuate.

If you've come to the end of this book realizing you're underprepared for the possibility of having to shelter in place, view that as a learning opportunity. As long as you realize that there's still work to be done, you've never failed, and every day in front of you is a day you can work on your emergency preparedness. For more details on how to prepare for bugging in, refer back to my previous titles, where you'll find much more detail about preparing your food stocks and other resources. And the bonus is, every extra detail you learn will help you with your bug-out plan too.

Being prepared is a never-ending journey. It's when we sit back and think we've got it all sorted that we're in trouble. There's always more you can do to make your plan better, and when you look at it that way, it's an adventure, and one you absolutely have the skills to embark on.

Always remember: Stay healthy; stay strong; stay prepared.

Ted Riley

Would your family survive in lockdown if society were to collapse? Learn how to prepare your home now.

We are used to a world in which our homes are supplied with fresh water, gas, and electricity.

We're used to having our waste removed and our sanitary needs met.

These are all things we've come to expect, but what would happen if they were taken away?

Flooding, hurricanes, and pandemics are affecting areas we once thought were safe from disaster--we shouldn't take anything for granted.

In *When Crisis Hits Suburbia: A Modern-Day Prepping Guide to Effectively Bug In and Protect Your Family Home in a Societal Collapse,* you'll learn exactly what you need to know to prepare your home for an emergency. You'll find:

- The **6 key priorities of survival** and how to make sure you have them covered

- A clear guide for knowing when it's time to stay in, and when it's time to evacuate
- Top prepper **survival secrets** so that you always stay one step ahead of the rest
- A toolbox of information that allows you to choose what works best for your family
- **Practical tips** for preparing your children for worst-case scenarios without frightening them
- How to make sure your water supply is 100% safe at all times
- Comprehensive checklists for everything you need to stock in your home
- **Essential administrative tasks** you should have sorted in advance before a disaster strikes

And much more.

The ideal home is not only the home that keeps you and your family safe in good times, but it's the home that **keeps you safe no matter what.**

Prepare your home for the worst-case scenario and protect your family no matter what.

Do you know how to stay healthy in the face of an emergency? Prepare now to keep your immune system on your side, no matter what happens tomorrow.

The chances of being stuck in our homes for long periods of time are greater than ever, and when disaster strikes, it can be difficult to get hold of crucial supplies.

Preppers have been evangelizing about food preservation and stockpiling for years. It turns out **they were right**, and now it's time to learn their secrets.

In *The Prepper's Pantry: Nutritional Bulk Food Prepping to Maintain a Healthy Diet and a Strong Immune System to Survive Any Crisis,* you'll find a **comprehensive guide** to preparing for good health in the face of an emergency. You'll discover:

- The **#1 way to stay healthy**, no matter what disaster is thrown your way
- Solid nutritional foundations for good health and strong immunity
- The importance of immune health in the event of an emergency

- 4 crucial food preparation **techniques** you'll need to adopt in order to stock your pantry efficiently
- A fool-proof guide to shopping, preparing, and storing your stocks for safe-keeping
- What **cupboard essentials** you should get a hold of now, and how to prolong their shelf-life
- **Lost skills** previous generations had down to a fine art, yet how you can pick these up once again

And much more.

You won't just be preparing to survive: **you'll be preparing to thrive**.

Know exactly how to prepare for good health in the face of a crisis.

You can stockpile all the rice you like... but do you know how you're going to cook it if you're without power for months on end?

If the power grid fails, it's not just your lights that go out. It's your water supply. It's your heating and cooling system. It's all your usual ways of cooking food or doing the laundry.

Without the grid, life as we know it changes in an instant.

Are you prepared for that?

In *Prepare Your Home for a Sudden Grid-Down Situation,* you'll discover:

- The most likely causes of a grid-down situation -- and how they'll affect your family
- **Easy immediate short-term solutions to see you through the first few days of disaster**
- Grid-down cooking options (you'll be amazed by how many ways there are to feed your family a delicious hot meal without your cooker)
- **A full range of emergency backup solutions you can fall back on if you're currently totally reliant on the grid**

- What to do when cash means nothing -- think outside the box to make sure your family thrives
- **The ultimate guide to making sure your family has access to clean, safe water (no matter what's going on outside)**
- Exactly what you can do to stay healthy and well when the toilet won't flush, the washing machine's useless, and a long hot bath is out of the question
- Everything you need to know about communicating with the outside world in a grid-down emergency
- **A clear breakdown of your off-grid power options -- so you can plan now for any unexpected event**
- Easy DIY projects you can work through right now to sharpen your skills and prepare for the worst

And much more.

If you thought your stash of canned beans and laundry supplies was enough to see you through an emergency, think again. It's a great start... but have you thought about how you're going to cook those beans? Do you know how you're going to wash your clothes?

Being prepared is about more than stocking up. It's about thinking outside the box and learning essential survival skills.

If you haven't already, don't forget to access your free
Emergency Information Planner

Follow the link below to receive your copy:
www.tedrileyauthor.com
Or by accessing the QR code:

You can also join our Facebook community **Suburban Prepping with Ted,** or contact me directly via ted@ tedrileyauthor.com.

REFERENCES

Bobby. (2013, July 29). *Inspirational learning and training quotes | SkyPrep*. Online Training Software | Award-Winning LMS | SkyPrep. https://skyprep.com/2013/07/29/15-inspiration-learning-and-training-quotes/

Brower, H. (2023, January 19). *14 martial arts for survival and prepping*. Survival Sullivan. https://www.survivalsullivan.com/find-right-self-defense-class-preppers/

The bug out bike—Bicycling survival when the SHTF. (2016, September 6). UK Preppers Guide. https://www.ukpreppersguide.co.uk/the-bug-out-bike-bicycling-survival-when-the-shtf/

Bug out cabin tips | How to build the ultimate survival shelter. (2014, October 20). American Gun Association. https://blog.gunassocia tion.org/how-build-bug-out-cabin/ #Tips_for_Building_a_Bug_Out_Cabin

Build a Bugout motorcycle. (2021, June 25). Prepper.com. https://prep per.com/bugout-motorcycle/

C, M. (2021, May 10). *7 Kickass booby traps that keep intruders on their toes*. Tactical Blog | Tactical Gear Reviews. https://www.tactical. com/booby-traps/

C, M. (2022, April 4). *Bugging out on foot: Do you have what it takes?* Tactical Blog | Tactical Gear Reviews. https://www.tactical.com/ bugging-out-on-foot/

Canadian Prepper. (2021, May 13). *A Prepper's guide to strength & fitness training for the Apocalypse*. Canadian Preparedness. https://canadian preparedness.com/blogs/news/a-prepper-s-guide-to-strength-fitness-training-for-the-apocalypse

Chymiy, A. (2018, May 25). *Physical fitness for preppers*. The Prepared. https://theprepared.com/prepping-basics/guides/survival-fitness/

City Prepping. (2020, August 26). *7 tips for bugging in an apartment*. https://www.cityprepping.com/2020/08/26/7-tips-for-bugging-in-an-apartment/

Cobb, J. (2022, January 15). *6 street smart skills you need in an urban disaster*. Urban Survival Site. https://urbansurvivalsite.com/6-street-smart-skills-you-need-in-an-urban-disaster/

Coffman, S. (2016, June 29). *4 foolish mistakes people make when picking a 'bug-out' location (LOTS of people do No. 2)*. Off The Grid News. https://www.offthegridnews.com/extreme-survival/4-foolish-mistakes-people-make-when-picking-a-bug-out-location-lots-of-people-do-no-2/

Cowbell, M. (2015, June 15). *Waterproof underground PVC cache*. Instructables. https://www.instructables.com/Waterproof-Underground-PVC-Cache/

Data storage for Preppers. (2017, May 1). The Prepper Journal. https://theprepperjournal.com/2017/05/01/data-storage-for-preppers/

Dzr, K. (2020, July 14). *Making cycling a part of your prepping*. The Prepared. https://theprepared.com/forum/thread/making-cycling-a-part-of-your-prepping/

Edwards, T., & Ward, S. (2022, May 18). *Rucking for exercise can boost strength, stamina, and power*. Healthline. https://www.healthline.com/health/fitness/rucking#how-to-get-started

Einsmann, S. (2021, October 15). *The best bug out bags for preparedness*. Outdoor Life. https://www.outdoorlife.com/gear/best-bug-out-bags/

Fishing licenses and regulations. (n.d.). America Go Fishing. https://www.americagofishing.com/fishing/fishing-licenses-and-regulations.html

G, J. R. (2020, February 26). *When to bug out: How to develop a complete bug out plan*. DIY Prepper. https://www.diyprepper.com/when-to-bug-out/

Hendry, K. (2021, July 6). *How to know when to bug out*. Survival Sullivan. https://www.survivalsullivan.com/how-to-know-when-to-bug-out/

Hobel, P. S. (2019, January 4). *Bug-out planning 101*. RECOIL OFFGRID. https://www.offgridweb.com/preparation/bug-out-planning-101/

Holecko, C. (2022, November 29). *The right way to play the classic outdoor game capture the flag*. Verywell Family. https://www.verywellfamily. com/how-to-play-capture-the-flag-1257384

How to build the ultimate survival cache—Mandatory supplies for SHTF. (2021, March 21). ReadyToGoSurvival. https://www.readytogosur vival.com/blogs/prepping-101/survival-cache

Hunter, J. (2022, October 13). *The practical guide to survival cache planning*. Primal Survivor. https://www.primalsurvivor.net/survival-cache/

James, D. (2022, October 6). *Are national parks good bug out locations?* SHTF Blog—Modern Survival. https://www.shtfblog.com/are-national-parks-good-bug-out-locations/

James, D. (2022, July 14). *Bug out communication gear and strategies*. SHTF Blog—Modern Survival. https://www.shtfblog.com/bug-out-communication-gear-and-strategies/

Jarhead Survivor. (2022, June 13). *Selecting a campground as a bug out destination*. SHTF Blog—Modern Survival. https://www.shtfblog. com/selecting-a-campground-as-a-bug-out-destination/

Joe. (2022, July 14). *Using a boat as a bug out location*. SHTF Blog—Modern Survival. https://www.shtfblog.com/using-a-boat-as-a-bug-out-location/

Jones, K. (2019, July 19). *Bug out or bug in—How to know when to go (or stay)*. The Provident Prepper. https://theprovidentprepper.org/bug-out-or-bug-in-how-to-know-when-to-go-or-stay/

Jones, K. (2019, September 13). *Steps to build a successful family emergency plan*. The Provident Prepper. https://theprovidentprepper. org/steps-to-build-a-successful-family-emergency-plan/

Just a moment... (n.d.). Just a moment... https://bugoutbagacademy.com/ free-bug-out-bag-list/

Just In Case Jack. (2021, September 16). *23 best prepping quotes from history to motivate & inspire*. Skilled Survival. https://www.skilledsur vival.com/best-prepping-quotes/

Kim, B. (2016, May 16). *Special needs Preppers: The elderly*. The Survival Mom. https://thesurvivalmom.com/special-needs-elderly-preppers/

Kirtley, P. (2014, December 21). *10 bushcraft & survival skills to try this winter.* Paul Kirtley. https://paulkirtley.co.uk/2014/10-bushcraft-survival-skills-to-try-this-winter/

Krebs, J. (2020, April 8). *How to use a compass and map.* The Prepared. https://theprepared.com/survival-skills/guides/learn-compass-map/

Levy, G. (2022, August 1). *A guide to building the perfect bug out bag.* Backdoor Survival. https://www.backdoorsurvival.com/how-to-build-your-own-perfect-bug-out-bag/

Loosli, L. (2020, September 30). *How to really secure your bug out location.* Food Storage Moms. https://www.foodstoragemoms.com/how-to-really-secure-your-bug-out-location/

M, R. (2020, December 12). *The cheapest way to build a sturdy, reliable bug-out retreat.* Off The Grid News. https://www.offthegridnews.com/extreme-survival/the-cheapest-way-to-build-a-sturdy-reliable-bug-out-retreat/

MacWelch, P. T. (2019, September 12). *Survival sanitation: Dealing with the "S" in SHTF.* RECOIL OFFGRID. https://www.offgridweb.com/survival/survival-sanitation-dealing-with-the-s-in-shtf/

Make a plan form. (2022, October 14). Plan Ahead for Disasters | Ready.gov. https://www.ready.gov/plan-form

Marlowe, T. (2022, April 23). *How to build a network of survival caches.* Survival Sullivan. https://www.survivalsullivan.com/survival-caches/

McCarthy, P. (2016, April 28). *Can conventional RVs work in a bug-out scenario?* RECOIL OFFGRID. https://www.offgridweb.com/survival/can-conventional-rvs-work-in-a-bug-out-scenario/

McCarthy, P. (2016, December 10). *Skivvy roll technique for efficient packing.* RECOIL OFFGRID. https://www.offgridweb.com/preparation/skivvy-roll-technique-for-efficient-packing/

McKoy, S. (2018, February 22). *Preparing for a disaster with a medical condition.* BugOut MAG!. https://www.bugoutmagazine.com/preparing-disaster-medical-condition/

Millerson, M. (2020, November 10). *Bug out bike.* Survive Nature. https://www.survivenature.com/bug-out-bike.php

Millerson, M. (2021, November 1). *All you need to know about a survival cache.* Survive Nature. https://www.survivenature.com/survival-cache.php

Mortensen, K. (2018, December 7). *The ideal diet for 4 year old kids.* Healthy Eating | SF Gate. https://healthyeating.sfgate.com/ideal-diet-4-year-old-kids-2221.html

Murphy, R. (2021, May 20). *Bug out location: 12 qualities of a safe bug out property.* PERSURVIVE. https://persurvive.com/bug-out/bug-out-location/

Perry, C. (2021, August 19). *Survival fishing 101.* The Prepared. https://theprepared.com/survival-skills/guides/fishing/

Planning a bug out route for emergency evacuation. (2016, December 24). Graywolf Survival. https://graywolfsurvival.com/1014/how-to-plan-bugout-route/

Planning your evacuation or bug out route. (2022, May 17). PREPARED-NESS ADVICE. https://preparednessadvice.com/planning-evacuation-bug-route/

R, A. (2019, September 17). *Bushcraft 101: Bushcraft tools and skills you should know.* Tactical Blog | Tactical Gear Reviews. https://www.tactical.com/bushcraft-skills-checklist-shtf/

Ramey, J. (2021, May 10). *Bug in vs. bug out: Why your home is always the default choice.* The Prepared. https://theprepared.com/prepping-basics/guides/bug-in-vs-bug-out/

Reaper. (2022, January 13). *How to test your bug out bag and bug-out range.* Survival Sullivan. https://www.survivalsullivan.com/test-bug-bag/

Renee. (2021, November 17). *Bug out cabins: What they are and how to prep yours.* Survival World. https://www.survivalworld.com/preparedness/bug-out-cabins/

Rogue, M. (2020, August 17). *How secure is your bug out location?* SHTF Blog—Modern Survival. https://www.shtfblog.com/how-secure-is-your-bug-out-location/

Rucker, B. (2022, June 4). *Essential guide on how to learn to hunt (Tips for beginners).* Survival Cache. https://survivalcache.com/hunting-tips-beginners/

Ruiz, C. (2021, February 22). *How to make a bug out plan.* The Bug Out

Bag Guide. https://www.thebugoutbagguide.com/how-to-make-a-bug-out-plan/

Smyth, B. (2021, July 6). *The essential guide to building your ultimate bug out bag*. Task & Purpose. https://taskandpurpose.com/gear/how-to-build-the-ultimate-bug-out-bag/

SpecificLove. (2015, February 19). *How to make a mousetrap trip wire alarm*. Instructables. https://www.instructables.com/How-to-make-a-Mousetrap-Trip-Wire-Alarm/

Stewart, M. (2018, December 27). *How to bug out if you have children*. The Survivalist Blog. https://www.thesurvivalistblog.net/advice-on-bugging-out-with-children/

Sullivan, D. F. (2022, August 16). *Bug out location: How to find and equip it*. Survival Sullivan. https://www.survivalsullivan.com/bug-out-location-dos-donts-and-the-basics/

Sullivan, D. F. (2022, December 26). *The best 37 survival foods to hoard for any disaster*. Survival Sullivan. https://www.survivalsullivan.com/the-ultimate-37-foods-to-hoard-for-any-disaster/

Survival 101: Foraging for edible plants. (2014, March 17). Be Prepared - Emergency Essentials. https://beprepared.com/blogs/articles/survival-101-foraging-for-edible-plants

Survival Dispatch Staff. (2019, December 10). *Using an abandoned building for shelter*. Survival Dispatch. https://survivaldispatch.com/using-an-abandoned-building-for-shelter/

Tilford, A. (2021, May 13). *Many Americans don't have an emergency go-bag*. Insure.com. https://www.insure.com/home-insurance/emergency-go-bag-survey/

Voh. (2021, September 18). *Increase in natural disasters on a global scale by ten times*. Vision of Humanity. https://www.visionofhumanity.org/global-number-of-natural-disasters-increases-ten-times/

Vuković, D. (2022, October 11). *9 crucial prepping tips for the elderly*. Primal Survivor. https://www.primalsurvivor.net/prepping-tips-elderly/

Vuković, D. (2022, October 13). *Bug out bag first aid kit list: What you need*. Primal Survivor. https://www.primalsurvivor.net/bug-out-bag-first-aid-kit/

Vuković, D. (2023, January 9). *Complete guide to dog bug out bags and bugging out with a dog.* Primal Survivor. https://www.primalsurvivor.net/dog-bug-out-bag/

Vuković, D. (2023, February 2). *The ultimate bug out vehicle checklist.* Primal Survivor. https://www.primalsurvivor.net/bug-vehicle-checklist/

Walter, J. (2018, September 8). *Bug in or bug out: When to run and when to stay.* SuperPrepper.com. https://www.superprepper.com/bug-in-or-bug-out/

Walter, J. (2018, July 11). *How to find the ultimate bug out location (BOL).* SuperPrepper.com. https://www.superprepper.com/choosing-a-bug-out-location/

Walton, J. (2018, March 22). *If you see these 6 signs it's time to Bugout.* Ask a Prepper. https://www.askaprepper.com/if-you-see-these-6-signs-its-time-to-bugout/

Weston, J. (2018, October 31). *Prepper fitness for self defense: Training for survival.* Backdoor Survival. https://www.backdoorsurvival.com/prepper-fitness-for-self-defense/

What is rucking? Complete guide to amazing benefits & more. (n.d.). GORUCK. https://www.goruck.com/pages/what-is-rucking

Wiley, S. (2012, May 7). *Bugging out with kids.* The Shooter's Log. https://blog.cheaperthandirt.com/bugging-kids/

Williams, C. (2022, October 17). *Ultimate guide to bug out vehicles: How to prepare for when SHTF.* Vinjatek. https://vinjatek.com/bug-out-vehicles/

Yor, C. (2022, November 6). *Bug out routes: Figuring out your evacuation paths.* Survival Sullivan. https://www.survivalsullivan.com/route-planning/